How to go Broke with Style:

A User's Guide to Filing (or Avoiding) Bankruptcy
with Humor & Grit!

Authored by Miss Ing Denero

ISBN 987-0-557-24864-3

This book is dedicated to my son, who was with me on the journey...and sometimes blazed the trail.

PREFACE

At the urging of several friends, I have decided to share my story. This is not a fairy tale (although a happy ending is certainly NOT out of the question!) Instead, it is the real life tale of how I went from making over $220,000 a year to being broke—and what I have learned along the way. My only purpose in telling my story is that what I've experienced may help you in your journey to survive and stand tall through a potentially demoralizing process.

When things started really going south in early 2008 and I started looking around for help, I found very little. Bankruptcy was the 'dirty little secret' of the suburbs then. Shortly after, a tidal wave began to emerge with the mortgage crisis becoming front-page news. Since then, several large corporations who previously appeared infallible have crumbled, while still others have been bailed out by the government. The tidal wave has evolved into an economic tsunami. Other companies have succumbed to economic doom and many are doing their part to make bankruptcy more mainstream every day.

Still, there is very little "user friendly" information out there for the average consumer embarking on this journey. In my search for answers, all I found were very dry "how-to" books written by attorneys and accountants about the tactical side of bankruptcy...not really helpful if you're still trying to decide how to survive!

When I shared my situation with a few close friends, I found an ever increasing circle of people I knew who were in similar situations. What a shock! I was quickly becoming the 'go to' person for questions about what to do, what happens next, where to get help, etc. So it made sense to me that a friendlier version of how you might go through the process without losing your mind...and your sense of humor...might be appreciated.

Let me first say that this book is not for the faint of heart. My philosophy of life is demonstrated on my bumper—my car bumper, to be more specific (see front cover). Life IS too short...and even the bible tells you to be bold! Most importantly, rules truly are made to be broken...at least some of the time. I am one of those "take a bite out of life" kind of people...I believe in asking for forgiveness instead of permission. And most of all, I live by the motto I have on a sign in my office...

"Life is not a journey to the grave with the intention of arriving safely in a pretty & well preserved body, but rather to skid in broadside, totally worn out & proclaiming...

WOW, What a Ride!"

That being said, YOU do not have to be a daredevil. This book is simply the telling of how I experienced this process, complete with triumphs, missteps & the resulting affects of all those actions. Mine is an extreme case, with lots of debt from a previous company and no real income to sustain me. Some things may ring true to you, while others may not apply. And it is important to say that I am NOT AN ATTORNEY!!! My hope is simply that you will come away with a basic understanding of what happens when you run out of money and the creditors start calling.

Please note that this is a journey of going broke...NOT of losing everything. Yes, I have had to learn to live without a lot of the creature comforts that I once deemed essential to my being. However, my friends, my family, meaningful work, my health & my God—and, yes, even my sense of worth—are all still in my possession.

You may notice some familiar song references in the chapter titles of this book. You are not mistaken! Allow me to explain. For most of my life, I have had the uncanny ability to subconsciously articulate my mood in song. I'll find myself absently humming a tune... then suddenly, I'll realize that the song's title or lyrics perfectly describe my current situation or thought process!! I KNOW!! And while I am a not a huge fan of the Beatles, I have found myself humming their tunes a lot lately...they really seem to fit! So with apologies to the Fab Four...here's to *Going Broke with Style!*

TABLE OF CONTENTS

EPILOGUE 2012

Here's to...

Going Broke with Style!!!

CHAPTER 1

"I Should Have Known Better"

How Someone with an Executive Level Background Got Herself into this Mess to Begin With!

This is the story of a girl with a dream. You see, throughout 20+ years in corporate America, my dream was to be in business for myself. This dream was not about money...it was about a family legacy...and about control. I was raised by a serial entrepreneur—a man who never worked for anyone but himself throughout my entire lifetime. Growing up throughout the '60's & '70's with my father as my role model, I knew that someday I would be in control of my own fate. I worked for him starting as early as my freshman year in high school, working long hours and always being the last to be paid. But somehow I knew inside that it was worth it. If things went well, he could congratulate himself! If they didn't, he had nowhere else to look and no one else to blame. That type of existence has always appealed to me.

But as any good girl did in the early '70s, I packed up and went away to college. The generation of my sister and I was the first in our family to attend college (or graduate from high school, for that matter!). And in 1973, the few girls who went to college were there to either become a teacher or a nurse. Knowing I wasn't crazy about blood, I chose the latter…and I launched into getting a teaching degree.

Three short years later, just short of graduating, I found myself in a not-so-great area doing my student teaching. Here I witnessed hyperactive children being restrained to their chairs in the classroom and 6th graders extorting lunch money from their fellow students! During a conversation with one of the little criminals-in-training, I informed him that if his behavior didn't improve, I would have to call his mother. His quick retort…"Good luck, maybe you can find her." I knew that this wasn't going to be the career path for me…

So after a few quick stints in homebound/hospital bound teaching, I found myself applying for a job in retail. I still remember my first day on the job. I couldn't believe my luck! Why wasn't everyone doing this, I wondered??? I loved it from the moment I arrived each day until I went home at night. I was getting paid for this?? I spent exactly three months as a location manager before I was promoted. Now, as an area manager, I had even more control of my time and I was mobile! I was getting paid to go all over the greater Chicagoland area to visit shopping malls! You have to be kidding me!

Things progressed at a rapid rate. Within a few months, I was asked to travel to other states to help district managers having trouble. Within the year, I was asked to take on the job of district manager in Detroit, as the existing manager had left unexpectedly...she had contracted a rapidly progressing case of non-lymphoma leukemia, from which she succumbed less than a year later. Still feeling invincible, I rapidly accepted—even though I was married and living in Chicago. As my husband (at the time!) was unable to relocate, the company rented me an apartment, bought me a company car and sent me to live in Detroit Monday through Friday, flying back home to Chicago every weekend.

I could not believe that my services could render such a generous reaction from my employer! I lived this tale of two cities for over two years—a single, all expenses paid life during the week, then flying home to be married on the weekends. Strange as it was, I loved it...even though it was a very strange existence. Imagine looking for something in your closet... and not knowing whether it was at the drycleaners...or in a closet in another city! Even though it stretched what should have been a two-year marriage into an eight-year one, I wouldn't recommend the lifestyle. I let years sweep away...

But you see how I got sucked in....my success in making numbers happen got me promoted quickly and often. I was a regional manager by age 27, supervising district managers (mostly men—it was the 80's after all!) who were 10+ years older than me with homes and families! Now instead of driving around, going to malls and having coffee with people, I was flying around, going to malls and having breakfast, lunch and dinner with people…all on the company dime. I was living high, flying on corporate jets and making lots of money.

This trend continued until somewhere in the early 90's when I finally realized that I did not have a life. People would talk to me about current events, and I was clueless. My life was the numbers, my travel schedule and living the corporate life. Having racked up one divorce, I was newly single at age 30 and still getting promoted. Sure, I enjoyed the single life—and was recruited to be part of a well-known retailer going through an LBO (leveraged buy-out) and just hitting its stride on the national scene. Now I was managing an area that included half of the United States, including Hawaii. I moved to California and got sucked back in…I was living the life! My first home was in Malibu, where the ocean view was at my doorstep.

In the midst of it all, I met someone on a beach in Hawaii and fell in love. I was there working…he was living there and surfing (guess that should have been a clue!!). But I fell hard and fast for this hard body who couldn't get enough of me.

We traveled across the ocean several times to see each other, which was expensive and frustrating! He wanted me to give up my job and move to Hawaii, but as career driven as I was, I just couldn't envision it! So he left the beautiful beaches of Hawaii and joined me in LA. I was still tracking, you see. Within a year, I had an offer on the East Coast—so we packed up and moved to New Hampshire. The good news was that this was a job that required much less travel, so I actually could pretend that I had an existence outside of work! The bad news was the (then) husband hated being away from the warm weather and beaches, so things started going south on a personal level pretty quickly. But hey, I rationalized, I was making a lot of money!!! Hmmm....

About a year after our move to the most conservative state in the nation, I found myself almost 40 and pregnant! Yeah, you know the jokes...but I was almost 40 AND pregnant!!! At first, I was really taken back, as I had not ever really thought much about having a child. But then my sister said to me..."You take the gift when it is given." It all started to make sense. For most of my adult life I wasn't even able to keep a houseplant, let alone a pet...or anything that would require my presence to take care of! But now I was on the road only a few months of the year and married. This might just work!

On September 29, 1994, I gave birth to my son, who remains to this day the entire light of my life. He has given meaning to everything I do, and quickly set about helping me get my priorities in order. Don't get me wrong...I didn't change completely overnight. My son's first executive board meeting was on his 6th birthday…his 6th DAY birthday! I had to come into the office for a "can't miss" meeting…and the company's president held my son for the first hour of his presentation. I thought perhaps I could figure things out!

Now that my son was my primary focus in life, I was led to embrace a very different set of priorities. Traveling became almost impossible, as I couldn't bear to leave him. Within the first year of his life, I met someone on a plane who eventually offered me a job to move to Atlanta where I could be home almost every night. With my marriage on the rocks and an opportunity to start over in a warmer climate, I moved the two of us to Atlanta just before Thanksgiving in 1995.

Don't think I was sacrificing….this job allowed me to be home every night because I had access to company jets that would take me where I needed to be—no lines, no waiting at airports. This led to some very last minute arrivals at his day care's Christmas plays and other festivities, but I was home more than I had ever dreamed possible.

This lasted until early 1997, when I was laid off for the first time in my life. I had been in charge of new business development, and the company had set its sights on a competitor. The program executed under my tenure was so successful, that the competitor acquiesced…and was bought out by my employer. I had successfully worked myself out of a job.

Wouldn't you think I would have learned my lesson by then?? But no—I simply put the house on the market and started a search for my next corporate gig. About a month into my search, I got a call from a recruiter about an opportunity to run a company back in the northeast. It was to require a lot of hard work, reorganizing, etc., but would include an equity position with a golden parachute that would leave me with a potential pot at the end of the rainbow in about 10 years. I couldn't wait! I called a dear friend and confidant to tell him the great news. His response…"Who is going to introduce you to your teenage son in 10 years?" Ouch. Hard to hear, but true. I started that day with plans to finally control my own destiny….

When I officially left corporate America in 1997, I was bringing home salary & bonuses that totaled over $220,000 a year. Yep…and that was over 12 years ago. I knew that I was never going to match that kind of income working for myself, but I was willing to make the necessary changes to call my own shots. So in early 1997, I set about on my path to entrepreneurialism—a path I've managed to stay on ever since.

You may wonder why I am filling you in on my life long before bankruptcy. My purpose is simply this….I would have never dreamed that I would end up here. Of all the potential outcomes I had envisioned for myself, going completely broke never even entered into my sphere of awareness. I knew that perhaps someday I would have to go back and get a "real job"…but never ever ever did I think that I would lose my house, my car, my dignity by finally giving in. But it happens. And nowadays, it seems to happening to more and more people.

They say misery loves company, but knowing that other previously successful people have landed in the same situation as me gives me little comfort. I just wanted you to know that previous income, former status and strong work ethics do not exclude you from this non-exclusive club.

And now, back to our regular programming…

My first visit to a bankruptcy attorney was horrible. I had waited too long and nearly all the money was gone. You see, I am not one of those calculating individuals who headed for bankruptcy with a plan. I wasn't smart enough to decide on bankruptcy early on and then work towards maximizing my options. You've heard stories, people who work to transfer assets to their spouse (or someone else), keep the debt in their name, then declare bankruptcy with their home and many of their creature comforts in tact. I guess I'm just not that smart! Or that devious…

In 2007, I closed on the sale of a business just in time to cover the last payroll. While the sale price looked like a big number, nearly half of the proceeds went to pay off debt secured by the assets of the business. And that was just the secured debt. Personal loans and credit card debt tied to the business still loomed large. I walked away from the sale with $83,000 in my pocket and still $225,000 in debt.

Yet despite the obviously overwhelming nature of my situation, I still somehow thought I could stave off bankruptcy! You see, I thought I could fix it! (Must have some male genes in my biological mix, eh?). Because of my strong-willed nature, I plodded along for nearly 8 months, watching the proceeds from the sale of my business quickly drifting away. Here's the unbelievable part...I was NEVER late on a payment!!! Even with over $225,000 in unsecured debt, my credit score was still a tolerable 625!

With 25 maxed-out credit card accounts now bearing interest rates as high as 36.99%, I continued to pay the minimums on each account every month. And keeping current on these was no small task, by the way.

Basically, I had a (non-paying) part time job as my own accountant, starting each day determining which bills were due and figuring out how to pay them. And I became an expert on cut-off times at all the banks so I could make my bank runs on time. It was a horrible existence.

Then came the killing blow. In early 2008, a loan that I had carried for the buyers of my business defaulted...and that was it. That was my tipping point. We settled for a small percentage of the total amount they owed me, and suddenly I had no monthly income. To that point, I had been pouring all my time and energy into a new business venture (while I wasn't balancing what was left of my money!) Now, with nearly all of the money from the sale proceeds gone and the incoming trickle from the loan payment disappearing unexpectedly, I came to the realization. It was time.

My first call was to Consumer Credit Counseling Services. As you may have guessed, the legitimate services have been inundated since the downward spiral in the economy has accelerated. Their process is to register you, then have you complete a VERY long, very comprehensive questionnaire detailing your debt line by line, complete with balances, current interest rates and creditor information. Not fun. The good news is that I was able to do much of the work online, so I completed the forms and scheduled a call with one of their counselors. Because of their backlog, their earliest available call time was over a week away. So I waited.

On the scheduled day, the counselor called promptly at the appointed hour. She was pleasant and kind, but stared in disbelief at both the amount of my indebtedness and the on-time status on every account. We muddled through the set up of a program to reduce monthly payments and interest rates on just about every credit card account. It was clearly something I should have done months before.

We went through every credit card and account laboriously detailing the information. Once we were through the stack, it was determined that several interest rates would be drastically reduced! I had been paying over $4,600 a month in total payments on all remaining debt (crazy, isn't it?) Now, a single payment of $3,526 was to be made to the agency every month, from which they would distribute payments to each creditor who agreed to the revised terms. Based on their history with one of the accounts, they predicted that the interest rate would be reduced to 0% on at least two of my outstanding credit card balances! It was amazing. I thought I was going to make it!

So the credit counseling agency set about the process of mailing letters to all of my creditors informing them of my enrollment in the debt payment plan to document their agreement. And therein lies the rub! They MAILED the letters...as in U.S. Mail! I made my first payment at the beginning of February in lieu of paying any credit card minimums. They mailed the letters to the creditors, waiting for confirmation prior to commencing the payment plan. So we waited....

Can you see where this is going? It took over a month for some of the correspondence with the credit card companies to go back and forth. In the meantime, no payment was made (because confirmation of new terms had not been received!). All of the accounts that I had worked so hard to keep current for the past three years suddenly began to show 30 days (or more!) past due! In one month, my carefully guarded credit score went from 625 to 500. The tight rope that I had been walking for over two years had finally frayed to the point of breaking, taking me and my credit score to the pavement.

It was at that point that I began considering bankruptcy as an alternative. My credit score was now suddenly in the tank, plus I was on a five-year plan paying $3,526 each month to the credit counseling service! It finally occurred to me that filing bankruptcy was a better alternative. While the debt management program would remain on my credit report for the five-year term of the payments, my credit would only be affected for two years longer (a total of 7-10 years) under bankruptcy. The untenable monthly payments would go away…and it was looking like I wasn't' going to be able to afford them much longer anyway, as the new business still hadn't show many signs of life yet. I pulled out of the program after 3 months.

For the record, let me say that I strongly recommend talking to CCCS if you think you are in a somewhat salvageable position. For example, if you have regular income and a debt load that could reasonably be expected to be paid off over a 3-5 year period, it is certainly worth a try. I've recently heard that as a general rule, if your total debt is equal to more than half of your annual income, then bankruptcy should be considered. I would urge you to check out Consumer Credit Counseling Services (http://cccsinc.org), a national network of non-profit credit counseling agencies that can really help you if you are still helpable! There's a lot of phonies out there...these guys are the real deal.

So, back to the first attorney visit. With no friends in the biz (of bankruptcy), I did what every red-blooded American would do—I watched TV. You know those big firms who advertise on late night saying they specialize in helping people with excessive amounts of debt? You guessed it...that's where I went.

When I called to make an appointment, I was very surprised that they had openings on any day that I chose! (Little did I know that they scheduled appointments every 30 minutes, so they could jam in LOTS of appointments in on any given day!) I dutifully completed the required forms prior to my first meeting with the attorney. It was a painstaking process of listing every debt, every account number, every debtor name & address, every balance due--a process very similar to the one I had recently completed for the credit counseling service. Ouch. Feeling depressed all over again, I entered the small office, only to see an elderly couple exiting, the woman weeping. Grrreeeaaaatttt! I feel better already!

After I entered the attorney's office, he pulled out a form and asked me several rapid-fire questions about my situation. As mine was apparently not the typical story (read, I had absolutely no income and an excessive amount of debt!), the answers took longer than he had expected. His frustration was evident. He never even asked to look at the paperwork I had completed. I was out the door in less than 20 minutes.

I have since learned that these guys are referred to in the trade as "bankruptcy mills". You know those pitiful stories you see on the news about raids on puppy mills, complete with pictures of the neglected dogs herded into cages and left to fend for themselves? Yup, that's what happens. They know just enough to handle the average case and give run of the mill advice (pardon the pun), but after 4 visits, I finally figured out that these guys didn't have the expertise or the patience to handle my situation. I wasted valuable time. Don't use them.

After consulting a string of attorneys I had worked with in the past on other issues, I finally received a recommendation for someone adept at handling situations like mine. It doesn't hurt that he is also compassionate, informed, extremely helpful and gives me as much time as I need. And here's the best part...he will end up costing me the same amount as the "mill" guys. Lesson learned.

Types of Bankruptcy

So now it begins...the mashing of numbers that helps you decide which type of financial suicide you will choose. What set of circumstances would lead you to choose bankruptcy? The answer is this...you don't choose it—it chooses you. In other words, for the average Joe (or Josephine!), I don't think that bankruptcy is anyone's end game. This is certainly not to say that there aren't those unscrupulous individuals who see it as the easy answer (see above!). However, most honest, hardworking Americans land there because of an event or events that didn't turn out the way that they planned. Even worse, the curse of being conscientious and smart leads some of us to put our heads down and continue down the path of trying to figure things out when we should be asking for help!

Being in debt, big serious debt, is much like an insidious disease; it comes over you slowly and continues to creep into your soul until you wake up one morning and you are drowning in it. How's that for an uplifting analogy? If you have been there...or are there now...you know exactly what I mean.

Bankruptcy is that state of being where what you owe is greater than what you have. Pretty simple on the surface...not so simple when you're there! So if you have $20,000 worth of equity in your house (ha!) and owe $15,000 in credit card debt, you probably don't qualify (but remember, I'm not an attorney!!).

EVERYTHING you have and everything you owe is considered. It's kind of like a balance sheet for the "company" that is you.

Essentially, there are two types of bankruptcy (remember again, I am NOT an attorney...this is my understanding from a layman/woman's perspective!).

Chapter 13 is apparently the most common. Chapter 13 is the personal version of the ever-popular Chapter 11 you hear so much about these days with corporations. This is a "reorganization" type of bankruptcy, where you put all your debts on the table (with a trustee in a courtroom!), and a repayment plan is developed. This can be as little as 0% of your debts...provided your situation is dismal enough—guess where I fit in! I was told that if I chose this, I could "reaffirm" my car...and possibly my house...but I would have to prove to the court that I could afford the ongoing monthly payments made to the court over a period of up to five years.

Oh, and did I mention that the bankruptcy attorney's fees are figured in this total also??? Payments are made in one lump sum each month to the court and payments are distributed to all of your creditors, including the guy that brought you to the dance. It is kind of like a recurring revenue/annuity payment plan for attorneys. No wonder they like Chapter 13 so much.

Chapter 7 is the granddaddy of all bankruptcies. This is where you say you are broke, owe lots of people lots of money, and can't afford to pay anyone back. Interestingly enough, the attorneys require payment up front for this type of filing. You can be sure that whichever poison you chose, the attorneys get paid. Again, you can reaffirm certain things, like your car & even your house, if you show that you can afford to make the payments. And did I mention that you have to be current on your mortgage in order to reaffirm that debt? For me, that would have totaled about $18,000 in late payments & fees to my mortgage company.

Not gonna' happen!

So off I go on the final leg of filing bankruptcy. But you knew that is where this was going! This is one of those books you read where the end is in the beginning...and the story is in the telling. The journey that I've been on is what may be helpful to you. Many people (most of whom are attorneys!) can help you once you've reached this point. My purpose here is to help you before you make that call by sharing what I have been through over the past couple of years as I entered into this financial tunnel. This is not a story of how I spent the money, but how I survived while trying to crawl back out.

May you find a rung or two of this ladder beneath your feet.

CHAPTER 2

"While My Guitar Gently Weeps"

How to Feel a Little Sorry for Yourself

Without Completely Giving UP!

The most backhanded compliment I have ever received came from my final bankruptcy attorney (remember, the good guy!). I'm taking it as a compliment, because I choose to. I'll leave your opinion to you! After looking over my dismal situation during my first visit, he closed the file, looked up at me and said, "Are you on some kind of medication?" I was shocked and asked him why he was asking me such a personal (and off track) question! His response, "After talking with you for the last hour, I would never have known how terrible your situation was!" See what I mean? Backhanded...but a compliment, none-the-less!

As a single mother, my priority has always been my son. As I said earlier, I spent over 20 years in executive positions where I was either traveling or unavailable to having a life. The gift my son gave me was the gift of life—mine and his. I immediately began looking at options to slow down, stop the travel and be his mom.

His father and I divorced when my son was less than a year old. The only reason that I mention this is by way of telling you that I have never received any type of support from my ex. Emotional, physical, financial...you name it, he held it back. So that is the backdrop that my story is told upon.

Soon after my son's birth, I relocated and changed (or should I say created!?) my life, eventually leaving corporate America and starting my own business. For over 8 years, things were great on the financial side. My lifestyle didn't encompass quite the same pizzazz that I had previously enveloped myself in...but I had a real life. I was now able to be home when my son got home from school and still make enough money to keep the house and provide for more than just basic needs. I was even crazy enough to start a new venture the week after 9/11 (Sept. 11, 2001). That is just how optimistic and enthusiastic I had become.

Somewhere around late fall 2005, things started to fall apart. Without boring you with unnecessary details, my financial picture had begun to change. Where money had flowed fairly freely to that point, I was now finding myself utilizing credit to purchase necessities. I had invested in a few businesses that didn't perform as expected, and I was forced to get creative to maintain status quo. "But never fear", I told myself...it was just a blip and I would get things back on track.

Oh the curse of smart people. Have you noticed that the smarter you are, the harder it is to throw in the towel? As incoming revenue in the business continued to dwindle into early 2006, I was confident that I would be able to figure things out! Certainly there was a way to stabilize the money and control the bleeding. I began to look for buyers for the businesses that were trending down year over year. Had I entertained any ideas of selling when things were going well? Of course not! But now, finding buyers was critical to the businesses' survival.

Then in May of 2006 I got an inkling that there was trouble with the company that I had employed to handle all my payroll processing. Having been unable to get them on the phone, I decided to drive over to their offices to see what was going on. I was met in the parking lot by the local Fox News affiliate, cameras rolling. Having been alerted to this unfolding situation, they had been attempting to gain entry to the office to interview the owner of the company. Two other small business owners were talking to them, being interviewed for a segment on that night's broadcast. This was not what I had expected.

Bottom line—the owner of the company had committed fraud. He had collected all the money for payroll and taxes from hundreds of small companies like mine, but hadn't paid the taxes to the IRS when they were due. Many of us had received notices from the IRS over the past several months, but had always been assured that they were in error. The owner of the payroll company even went so far as to show us "proof" that they had rectified the situation. But now, standing in the parking lot of their office with a microphone in my face, I knew that this wasn't going to be easily fixed.

When it was all said and done, the owner of the payroll company was convicted and sent to Federal prison for 6 years. Nice…but little comfort to those of us who sat together in the courtroom licking our wounds from the millions of dollars he had scammed from us. Here's the real kicker…the IRS prosecuted and convicted this man, but still wanted to collect the money owed for payroll taxes from all of us. You see, where the government is concerned, the payroll company does not have a fiduciary relationship that shifts the burden of the tax liability to him. We all still owed the back taxes AND penalties and interest to the IRS!

Even after providing reams of paper to document that the monies had been drafted from all of our accounts, the response was still that our businesses all still owed what hadn't been paid. For most of us, the number was in excess of $35,000 over a period of a year and a half.

Fast forward to early 2007. Personal credit cards, along with business lines of credit, were all maxed out. An intervening incident of employee credit card theft that left all my bank accounts frozen for over 30 days, coupled with the ongoing trend down in revenue put me in the position of needing to sell before I couldn't afford to stay open. By the time I closed on the sale of my last business venture in June of 2007, I needed the proceeds to cover that business's last payroll.

So I pick up my story in March of 2008. All the remaining proceeds of the sale were completely gone (remember, I had still been paying all those credit card bills every month!), my small monthly income from loan payments had disappeared with the default on the loan I held from an earlier business sale, and I was left with precious little cash and no foreseeable income flow from the new business. The CCCS program had consolidated my payments, but had completely decimated my credit score. Even for someone with a fairly high threshold for change and uncertainty, I felt like I had fought my last fight.

That month, I stopped paying everything. When I say everything, I mean I stopped playing the whack-a-mole game of paying minimums on all those outstanding credit cards whos balances were at or over the max. I stopped paying CCCS. I was going to have to retreat and regroup.

Delays in the new business venture continued to happen, deferring any hope of new cash rolling in. April of 2008 was the last mortgage payment I was able to make. Now I was really down to the basics...food, utilities, car payment...I was now doling out money like an old widow, conserving for what may come. This was certainly a change for me.

There is a saying that goes something like this,

"The man who has everything is free. You can imprison a man who has some and will sell his soul to keep it. Only when the man has nothing does he become free again". I was now in the later category, unsure about what was next, what to do, or where I would end up. Yes, getting out of bed was nearly impossible as those days stretched on. But get up I did.

I decided that this was not a time to crawl back in defeat. The passion I had for my new business was still strong...and my son was watching. Preaching & teaching are two different things. I had always told him that we are all in control of our own destiny, and, with the grace of God, anything could be survived. Now I needed to show him by example that you can endure tough times and come out on the other end.

My first big move was to join a meditation class. Going somewhere to focus on something other than my problems, even for only two hours a week, was a beginning. The class was nearly free, located through my health insurance company. (Good thing I took it when I did, because within two months, I wasn't able to even pay those premiums anymore and we were without insurance!).

Deep breathing and visualization, as corny as they may sound, really do provide you with an opportunity to reconnect with yourself. Worry is a useless and non-productive emotion...so I set out to do things that would help me avoid it as much as possible. I even started walking, eventually training for a 10k walk that I had aspired to participate in for more than 5 years (yes, I did it!!!). I even began a gratitude journal, to remind myself daily of the many blessings that God was bestowing on me still. It's amazing what you see when you are seeking it!

My point here is this--don't let this or any other set back knock you out. There is too much of life to live to allow anything or anyone to overtake who you are. Anything is possible...and there is nothing like being taken down to nothing to help you get that view back in perspective.

CHAPTER 3

"Please Mr. Postman"

Unsecured Debtors Can't Hurt You!

You can imagine that about the time my credit card payments stopped, the volume of letters in my mailbox went up proportionately. And calls...boy do we get calls... Credit card companies have certainly got the phone thing down pat. Just as soon as the first payment was 5 days late, the phone started ringing. And ringing. And ringing.

I chose not to answer. Ever. In my case, there really was nothing to discuss. I had no money, so discussing a settlement was fruitless. I knew I was headed towards bankruptcy, and I knew that would make the letters stop. What I didn't know at the time was that I wouldn't be filing for months, for reasons I'll explain in a bit. So my phone just continued to ring.

First, Some Rules:

You should know the rules about calling you. Debt collectors have the right to contact you at work or at home between the hours of 8 a.m. and 9 p.m. You can make them stop. You can verbally tell them that your employer doesn't allow those types of phone calls, and they are supposed to stop. You can also make them stop calling you at home. This is a little more involved, because you must contact them in writing. Any debt collector must provide you with written verification of the debt if you request it, along with the debt amount and the steps you can take to dispute the claim. Have them mail this to you. Their address information should be on any contact letters that they send to you. This will give you the information you need to send them written notification that you do not want to be contacted any longer. But be sure to send this certified/return receipt requested so that you have proof that they have received your notification.

The most important thing to remember is to tune out threats. No debt collector can send you to jail or garnish your wages or tell you their sending someone over to break your legs. Only the courts can garnish your wages or your bank account to settle a debt. So unless/until any debt collector/creditor sues you, threatening garnishment is simply a threat. So is threatening you or your family…or continuing to call you at work or home after you have given them legal notification to stop. If they do, you MUST report any violations and undo harassment! The Federal Trade Commission enforces the FAIR DEBT COLLECTION PRACTICES ACT, so you can—and SHOULD—file complaints with them at www.ftc.gov. You can also contact your state's Attorney General. Don't let them scare you into doing anything you are not ready to do.

If you're like me, you never intended to stiff anybody. But I have to admit that feeling bad about stiffing credit card companies was somewhat mitigated by the fact that they consistently raised the interest rates on my cards, even though I had remained current for years and years and years. As I said earlier, the interest on many of my cards were running as high as 36.99%-- even though I hadn't ever been late!!! You see, until very very recently, credit card companies were able to access information from all other credit card companies and could charge you their maximum rate even if you were never late on their credit card! Get it?

So if you were late on a Visa payment, MasterCard could access that information and also charge you their penalty rate. Real fair…isn't it? With all that shared information, who do you think had the advantage?

Finally, consumers had had enough! The bad economy became the tipping point that finally mobilized Congress to pass the Credit Card Act of 2009 in May. As of August 20th, 2009, the credit card companies must give any consumer a forty-five day notice of any changes to the rate or fee increases. This is an increase from the fifteen-day notice of prior law.

This new law also mandates a 21-day period for payment on a credit card, before the credit card company can assess late charges. Previously, credit card companies only gave consumers fourteen days for payment after mailing out the bill. Under the new act, this payment period will increase to twenty-one days to accommodate for postal delivery times. Imagine that...allowing consumers enough time to get the bill, make out the check and mail it without being late! This was a result of the outcry of many people who have ended up paying late fees or lost their lower rates for being late by only a few days, or sometimes even just one day.

Phase II of this law was originally to be enacted in February of 2010. Among other things, this part of the law prohibits increases in interest rates on debt already incurred (exiting balances). In other words, if you are carrying a balance of $10,000, the credit card company can advise you that they are raising your interest rate on NEW PURCHASES ONLY. The interest rate on your existing balance stays the same. Gosh...imagine that Congress has to litigate this kind of common business sense.

But here's the killer...with this impending law on the books, credit card companies have spent most of 2009 hiking up interest rates on millions of Americans to get the increase in before the February 2010 enactment. As a matter of fact, credit card companies behaved SO BADLY that Congress has now decided to move the date up on this phase of the bill...to December of 2009! It's hard to believe that Congress acted that quickly...but the pressure from consumers has really been vocalized!

Silence is golden!

Here was my solution. I disconnected all phone lines except for the one in my home office. That eliminated the constant ringing of the home phone, which generally set my jaw on edge. Then, I forwarded the remaining line to my cell phone, and placed my cell phone on silent...where it remains to this day. Any incoming calls that I recognized or knew, I would answer. All others went to voicemail. That way, anyone calling who needed me could always leave a message, and I was able to be responsive. The calls from creditors were often computer-generated calls that didn't even leave messages... at least in the beginning. I accomplished one major thing--my world quieted down a bit.

Over time, the pattern of the creditors became obvious. The letters I received were at first very aggressive, "You MUST call me back before 5pm today!!!" "This is an URGENT message" "Your failure to respond...", you get the message. One credit card company even went to far as to call my neighbor...YES, MY NEIGHBOR!!! Apparently they "Googled" my street address and found someone two houses down. And of course, this was the neighbor who lives to keep the other neighbors informed, if you know what I mean. I was outed to my neighborhood by National City.

Then, as suddenly as it began, the aggression went away! About two months into the process, the messages became helpful in nature. I began receiving letters telling me that it wasn't too late…there was still hope for me. Here is a copy of the <u>actual card</u> I received from one credit card company several months into the process. It's my favorite!

There's still hope.

Here's the inside:

June 13, 2008

████████████

We're not one to give up on you. We know you're better than this. And we want to share something with you...

You're not alone in being behind on your payments. Thousands of Americans are.

Some have lost their jobs. Or have experienced a family or medical emergency. Others have suffered a divorce. Or have had terrible accidents. Still others have simply mismanaged their money.

But here's something you should know. Many others are finding they can work their way out of debt by asking Discover Card for smaller payments...for lower interest rates... and for an end to "late payment" charges. Discover Card responds to their requests and we'll consider yours, too. Just pick up the phone and call us toll-free at ████████████

Even if you can't pay us now, we urge you to call today. You may be surprised at what we can do to help you resolve this debt.

Please call us at ████████████ We will listen.

Sincerely,
Carrie Bush
DFS Services LLC

P.S. Call Toll-Free ████████████ All our representatives are trained to help you. Office hours: Mon.–Thurs. 8:00 AM to midnight; Fri. 8:00 AM to 10:00 PM, Sat. 8:00 AM to 2:00 PM Eastern Standard Time.

This is an attempt to collect a debt and any information obtained may be used for that purpose.

DISCOVER

00000514

Isn't that special. By the way, don't ignore the P.S. "This is an attempt to collect a debt"!

So, over time, their patterns were fairly evident. You see, credit cards are UNSECURED credit. That means they have no leverage other than fear. They cannot come to your house and take back whatever you have purchased with the credit card. They cannot (legally anyway!) threaten to send over their Uncle Louie to "persuade" you to pay the bill. They can only use words...and only between the hours of 8 a.m. and 9 p.m...to convince you somehow that you must pay them. First, they are threatening, mean and manipulative. If they do not achieve their desired outcome, their tactics change.

As of 08/25/08, your credit card account is 125 days past due.

It's not too late to begin
to repair the damage to
your credit.

CHASE ◘

We're here to help.

We have options that
can work for you.

Take control of your debt.
Just call ▮▮▮▮▮▮▮▮.

▮▮▮▮▮▮▮▮▮▮

**Getting out of debt—
Solutions that work**

Talk to a Customer
Support Advisor at
Chase. They can often
help you with payment
options, including
payment plans.

Pay more than the
minimum due.

Consider alternate
money sources for
paying off debt—stocks,
bonds, savings account,
family and friends, etc.

Don't miss payment
due dates.

Plan a budget.

Waking up every day with debt on your mind isn't pleasant. You may feel
overwhelmed or not know where to begin when it comes to resolving your
finances It's not too late to get back on track, and Chase can help.

No one wants to deal with collection agencies.

When you have daily phone calls about your credit card debt, it just adds to your
stress about money. That's why we want to help you do something about your debt
before your account is turned over to a collection agency. Once that occurs, you
may not have as many options available to help you repay your debt with Chase.

Your first step to avoid getting further into financial trouble is to call us.

You want to be in control of your debt. Every payment you miss puts you further
away from financial peace of mind. Negative marks on your credit report can stay
there for seven years. And that may affect your ability to purchase things you may
need in the future a home, a car, an education   things that require good credit.

When you have control over your finances, you have control over your future. We
are here to help you. We've enclosed tips and valuable information to help put you
back in control and to start a stress-free financial future. Look on the back of this
letter for important information to help you improve your credit.

Call us today to begin repairing your credit. You have the power to change your
financial situation and you have the support of Chase to get you there.

We can't help you unless you get in touch with us. Call ▮▮▮▮▮▮▮▮ today.

Sincerely,

Rina Carroll

Rina Carroll
Customer Support Division

FC-LSM
LC-BUC45

Then, suddenly, they want to help you, to assure you that
there is a solution. They beg you to call them to try to work out a
payment plan…even offering to reduce the amount owed if you
would just respond.

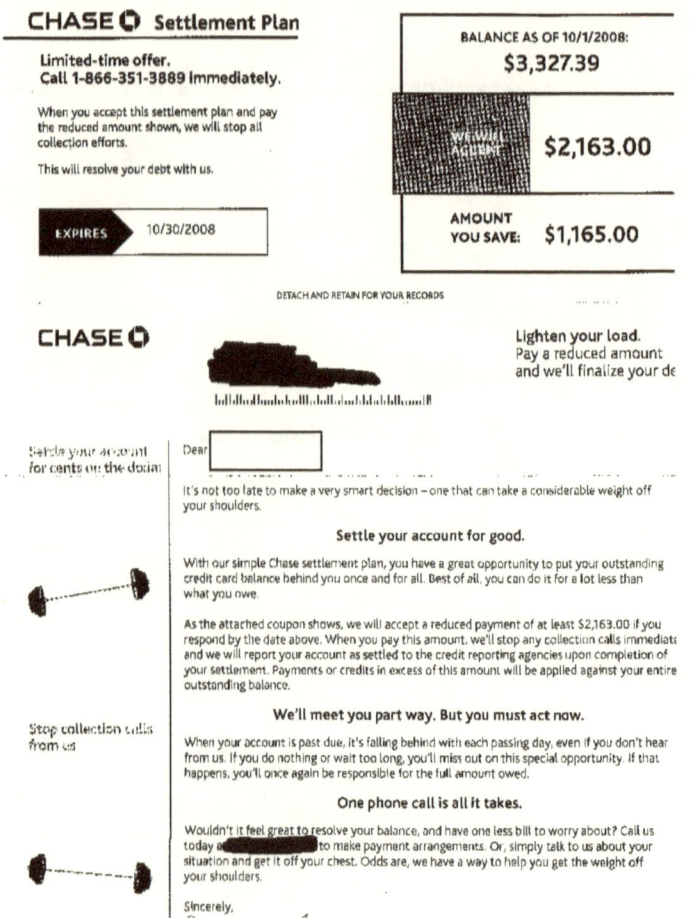

CHASE **Settlement Plan**

Limited-time offer.
Call 1-866-351-3889 immediately.

When you accept this settlement plan and pay the reduced amount shown, we will stop all collection efforts.

This will resolve your debt with us.

EXPIRES ▶ 10/30/2008

BALANCE AS OF 10/1/2008:
$3,327.39

WE WILL ACCEPT $2,163.00

AMOUNT YOU SAVE: $1,165.00

DETACH AND RETAIN FOR YOUR RECORDS

CHASE

Lighten your load.
Pay a reduced amount and we'll finalize your de

Settle your account for cents on the dollar

Dear

It's not too late to make a very smart decision – one that can take a considerable weight off your shoulders.

Settle your account for good.

With our simple Chase settlement plan, you have a great opportunity to put your outstanding credit card balance behind you once and for all. Best of all, you can do it for a lot less than what you owe.

As the attached coupon shows, we will accept a reduced payment of at least $2,163.00 if you respond by the date above. When you pay this amount, we'll stop any collection calls immediately and we will report your account as settled to the credit reporting agencies upon completion of your settlement. Payments or credits in excess of this amount will be applied against your entire outstanding balance.

We'll meet you part way. But you must act now.

Stop collection calls from us

When your account is past due, it's falling behind with each passing day, even if you don't hear from us. If you do nothing or wait too long, you'll miss out on this special opportunity. If that happens, you'll once again be responsible for the full amount owed.

One phone call is all it takes.

Wouldn't it feel great to resolve your balance, and have one less bill to worry about? Call us today at to make payment arrangements. Or, simply talk to us about your situation and get it off your chest. Odds are, we have a way to help you get the weight off your shoulders.

Sincerely,

This whole process takes about three months, but varies from creditor to creditor. But at some point, they give up any hope of getting their money out of you and sell your account to a collection agency. Then the entire process begins again. I believe that this goes on into infinity…the cycle of threatening Uncle Louie to trying to help, to selling to another tier of collection agency…and on and on and on. The only way to stop the swirling abyss is to either pay them or file for bankruptcy.

Based on my experience, here is a graphic showing the psyche & tactics of bill collectors:

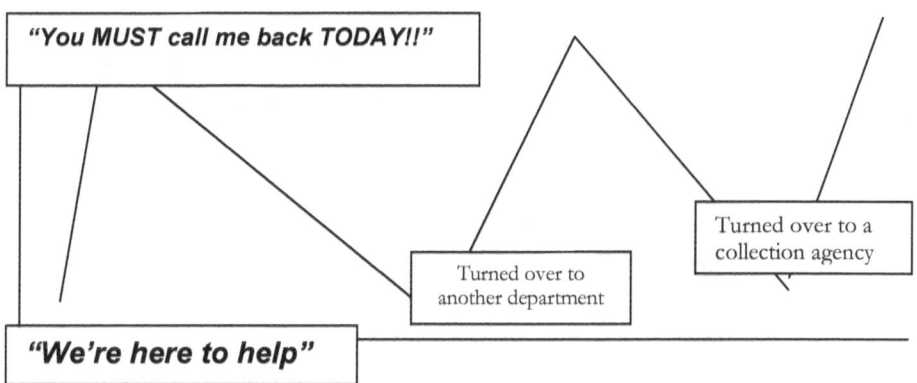

Timeline chart of Aggressive Collection vs. Helping Offers

As you can see, credit card collections is a lot like The Lion King...the whole "circle of life" thing. Within 5 days of being late on a payment, the calls came fast & furious. Aggression built like a crescendo until we reached the six to eight week point. Then they started to become my friends. They wanted to help. Couldn't we just work this out?

At some point, between two and three months, they sold the debt or escalated it to another department within their organization. Then the cycle started all over again. No more Mr. Nice Guy...."You MUST call me by 5p.m. today"..."This is an URGENT business matter"... yeah yeah yeah.

Yup, it is a roller coaster ride! But along the way, I received some very interesting appeals. Here are a few:

TELEWIRE ®
ELECTRONIC MESSAGE

P.O. Box 2983
Milwaukee WI 53201-2983

Content of This Message Created by Client, Not by Telewire
Printed & Mailed at Direction of Client by Telewire

August 25, 2008   014503

TEMP - RETURN SERVICE REQUESTED

RE: Kohl's Account Number 035069099652
Current Balance: $2257.38
Total Amount Due: $472.57

No Interest / No Fee Program

Dear   :

For a limited time, we are offering a No Interest / No Fee Program. Pay your current balance on your Kohl's charge account and receive no interest and no fees while in the program.

Qualifications:
* Simply setup 4 equal payments, over the next four months, that payoff your Kohl's Charge account.

* The four payments must be made with checks over the phone.

* All interest and fees on the account will be waived from the date the initial check was arranged until the 4th payment is completed.

To take advantage of this limited time offer or to discuss other available options in detail, you must call within 14 days of the date of this letter. We can be reached at ████████████. We are here every Monday through Friday, from 7:00 A.M. until 10:00 P.M., and Saturdays 7:00 A.M. until 4:00 P.M. (Central time).

Sincerely,

D.T. Erdmann
Assistant Collection Manager
Kohl's Corporate Offices

Then, nice went quickly to not so nice....

FIA CARD SERVICES™
www.FIAEasyPay.com

This Is Our Final Notice . . .

August 21, 2008

Dear

This is our final notice to you regarding the FIA Card Services, N.A. account(s) listed below. **You need to contact us by 10 p.m. Eastern time on August 28, 2008 otherwise these account(s) will be written off as a bad debt the next day.** After that, we will no longer be able to discuss these account(s) with you and we will likely sell them to a third party, who will begin collection efforts immediately.

Account:	Balance:	Payment Due:
	$11,689	$387
	$9,717	$290

In the event that your account is sold to a third party, they will continue to collect this balance from you and liquidate the account. This can be done in various ways such as phone calls, letters, and possibly legal action. You will no longer have the opportunity to work out the specific payment arrangements that FIA Card Services, N.A. has tried to resolve with you over the past several months. Remember, FIA Card Services, N.A. has had a long relationship with you, the third party who will handle your account has not.

Only you can prevent this from happening by calling **1-800-270-2870** and making a qualifying payment before 10 p.m. Eastern time. Time is running out!

Please call **1-800-270-2870**, Monday through Friday from 8 a.m. to 9 p.m., or Saturday, 8 to noon (Eastern time). Our knowledgeable Account Managers are ready to assist you.

Sincerely,

Brian Redmond
Senior Vice President

P.S. If you choose not to make payment arrangements, your relationship with FIA Card Services, N.A. will be terminated, however, you will still be responsible for this debt. (In addition, until the year 2014, any potential employer, mortgage company, car dealership, or creditor may be able to see this bad debt on your credit file.)

183RMFINNNAFXTCC
2744

And then, they became simply ridiculous! If you can believe it, I received more than one letter by FED EX OVERNIGHT MAIL…pleading with me to call them to settle! It seemed completely ridiculous to me…and apparently to them as well. Here's the actual label for the overnight package that was delivered to my door! Instead of the typical postage stamp, this must have cost them in excess of $14!!!

September 25, 2008

Account Number ending in: 6101

Dear

So you are probably wondering why we just paid to overnight you this one sheet of paper. Honestly, it is because we have not been able to contact you for some time and need you to call us so we can help you.

By not speaking with you, we have not had the opportunity to share with you a variety of solutions that may help you through whatever financial difficulty you may be experiencing. Let us help get your account back in good standing.

Simply put, there are a number of temporary and permanent options you may be able to take advantage of, including:

- ❖ Settling for less than your total balance. Payable in installments or all at once.
- ❖ Reducing your balance one time by an additional dollar for every dollar you pay us up to $599.
- ❖ Lowering your interest rate to reduce finance charges based on your call to us.
- ❖ Lowering your monthly payment based on your call to us.

In some cases we may even be able to combine options. It all starts with you making a phone ca today.

We are available to talk 7 days a week a████████████

Monday-Thursday 6:30 a.m. to 11:00 p.m. CT
Friday   6:30 a.m. to 9:00 p.m. CT
Saturday & Sunday 8:00 a.m. to 5:00 p.m. CT

You may also take advantage of select payment options at www.Citicards.com.

Sincerely,

G. Stevens
Vice President
Citicorp Credit Services, Inc. (USA)

PLEASE SEE REVERSE SIDE FOR IMPORTANT INFORMATION

0020-BC

CRITICAL POINT: If you think your situation is even remotely salvageable, THIS is the time to strike a deal!

When you find yourself at the low point of the cycle (the "we can help" stage)…MAKE A DEAL if you can afford to! (However…ONE BIG CAUTION--make sure you get everything in writing before mailing a check…and NEVER let them have access to your checking account information!!!)

This is the point when credit card companies realize that they really have no leverage and are willing to take whatever you can offer. You see, the worst case for them is what happened to me…I filed for bankruptcy and they were left holding the bag for the entire amount.

Believe me, it is not as pleasant for me as that may sound…I HATE that I was unable to make good on my debt. My son and I have had many conversations about exactly this point. I want him to grow up to be a man of honor, not someone who sees a way to use the system to his advantage. Those are lessons he will have to learn from my ex! (kidding, of course!!). But sometimes, you have to do what you have to do…and I was there.

CHAPTER 4

"We Can Work it Out"

You Can't Ignore a Lien on Your House...

But They Can Ignore You!

I stated earlier than I chose not to communicate. That was true for all those many credit cards representing unsecured debt whose representatives were persistently calling and sending letters. Secured loans are different. I took the exact opposite tact with my mortgage and my car...and a couple of lawsuits! Allow me to me explain.

As I saw myself heading for trouble in early 2008, I began a fairly aggressive communication program with the lender who held my mortgage. Because I had been self-employed for so long, I was one of those people who had obtained a loan based on stated income. I had refinanced in 2006, because I needed to cash out of some of the equity I had in my home of 10+ years. You remember, back when I was still trying to juggle without letting anything drop! Refinancing on stated income is now a thing of the past, but in 2006, it landed me in a VERY high percentage loan that was due to reset in mid-2008. In any possible scenario, I figured it was in my best interest to begin communicating with them as early as possible.

The first letter I sent was in April of 2008, shortly after mailing my last house payment. No response. In late April, I called. I was told very abruptly that there was no need to have a conversation now, as the loan was not due to reset for a few months and, frankly, they were so overwhelmed and behind that they would not be able to assist me until the date got closer. Hmmm....

In May, I called again. This time, I was a bit more aggressive and actually got a fax number and name in the "workout" department. They did inform me that this would not be a good use of my time, however, as my mortgage was current and in good standing. By May 15, I had fixed that problem. Now I was late, and I sent the letter.

June went by, then July....no word. Home values, and the economy, were dropping like a rock. Foreclosures, bankruptcies, failing stock prices all were the headlines. I called several times again, sent the same letter to the "workout" department again. Finally, at the end of July, I received a phone call. The individual asked me to fax the letter (again!!!), along with bank statements, etc. Now, he claimed, they were willing to talk.

Two days later an offer came back. They would reduce the interest on my mortgage by 2%--down to 7.75% from the current 9.75% that I was stuck in. There would be no discussion about the value of the home. And the loan would reset to a 40-year term. I'd be 93 before it was paid off. I declined.

I must say that I had a quite contrary experience with the company that held the loan on my car! During this same time period, what little cash I had on hand was dwindling fast, so I called them directly. Without hesitation, they told me of a plan they had for people in my situation. They agreed to let me skip one payment, then pay ½ payment per month for two months. I was amazed! No indignity! No yelling and screaming! They just asked me a couple of questions, completed the paperwork and mailed me the forms. You had better believe that I figured out how to pay those payments on time!

A car loan is also a secured debt, secured with the automobile in question. You don't want to ignore these guys either. I hear that the business of repossessing vehicles is doing well during the current economic downtrend...don't get caught by surprise!

The other bill that you have to take very seriously is your property tax bill. Yes, they can auction your house off for back taxes, but they do have to stand in line behind the mortgage holder. However, anyone who buys your house (through short sale or on the courthouse steps) will also be responsible for these taxes. That's why buying property at foreclosure sales is not for newbies who haven't done their homework.

The 2008 property tax bill came in November of 2008. It was due at the end of November, but I found out that it was not considered delinquent until February 15th of 2009 (I had to ask...I still thought I could figure it out at this point!!). Of course, I did not figure it out...and I have never once received another letter from my county tax assessor's office. Well, I take that back. I did receive one more letter....when taxes were due again for 2009. This...like many situations in my life, came with a bit of a twist!

The front page of local paper reported that one of our town's mail trucks had sort of instantly combusted while the carrier was making her deliveries one day in September of 2009. Of course, this was front-page news, as I live in a fairly small community. A photo of the incident was shown, chronicling the event. Much to my surprise, there was my old mail carrier! (We had since partially relocated, but were still receiving mail at the house). I felt so bad for her...she and I had become close as she delivered bad news to me daily over the previous several months—registered letters, attorney notices and the like.

I really didn't think too much more about it until one day I received a very strange letter wrapped in plastic in my new mailbox. You got it...my tax bill had caught on fire!!! What remained of the contents was salvaged, wrapped in plastic, mailed again—then forwarded to me at my new address. There has to some poetic justice or message in there…insert your own.

Here are photos of the evidence:

By August, I decided to list my house for sale with a broker who could assist me in a possible "short sale". At that time, I discovered that my house was now worth about 75% of the mortgage value. On a good day. I signed a letter authorizing my broker to speak with the lender on my behalf. Still no response.

As hard as I tried to communicate with them through this process, the mortgage company sat in almost complete silence. It was amazing. The largest debt that I had…for the home I had raised my son in for the past 12 years…and I couldn't even get anyone to return my call! I continued to receive normal monthly statements, stating the arrearages; I even received a letter about the upcoming resetting of the interest rate. I had not made a payment since April, and yet I heard nothing.

Laws differ from state to state (and, again, I am not an attorney!!!). However, in my state, laws heavily favor the lien holder. All they need to do is send you a registered letter and list your property in the "legals" section of the designated paper, and the house is auctioned off on the steps of the courthouse the first Tuesday of the following month. My letter came in September. That meant that the house would be advertised for 4 weeks in October, and then foreclosed on in early November of 2008. The time to file bankruptcy had come.

You may wonder why I waited so long. The answer is very simple. I had no money. By the end of summer of 2008, I had pretty much resigned myself to the fact that I was going to lose the house. And I knew that by filing, all the letters & unwanted phone calls from creditors would go away. But mine was a clear case of Chapter 7. As I stated in the first chapter, there is no payment plan to the courts like there is in a Chapter 13 bankruptcy. As such, attorneys want to be paid up front to file Chapter 7. No kidding. From a business perspective, it makes complete sense! From my point of view, they wanted money I didn't have. I may be the only person you have ever heard of who couldn't afford to file for bankruptcy!

But here's the other thing. If you file for bankruptcy BEFORE they auction your house on the courthouse steps, the clock immediately resets. If you file for bankruptcy on Monday, it stops a scheduled "court house steps" sale on Tuesday. So I chose to play a waiting game. Since my mortgage company had been so completely non-responsive, I decided to wait until they did communicate. By the time they sent the letter regarding impending foreclosure in September, I was 5 months behind. While it bought me time, it did not solve my problem.

And those pesky lawsuits I mentioned earlier. Both were quite unexpected…and came in the middle of the worst of times for me. The first was brought about by a family that I had once considered among my dearest of friends. Ha! The wife had been employed by me for over five years, throughout good times and bad. In the beginning, business was great and I did all I could to share the wealth of the bounty. I sent this entire family (husband, wife and son) on a trip to Paris. Later I sent the husband and wife on a cruise while I took their son and my son on a trip to Disney World. I have always considered myself to be the type of person who looks to share their good will with others, and this family was certainly the recipient of much. But it wasn't simply monetary. Over the years, our families grew very close...generally spending holidays together, vacationing together, etc. Our sons even called the other their "second mom"....we were together most of the time, both in and out of our working relationship.

The husband in this relationship was growing increasingly envious of what he thought must be a bountiful lifestyle with much to spare. After watching me purchase several businesses, both alone and with another partner, he insisted that if there were ever to be an opportunity to purchase another business, he wanted in. So when the next business became available, I went to them with the same deal I had negotiated with a previous partner. For an injection of $15,000, they would hold a 50% investment in the business without any obligation to incur ongoing expenses or be involved in running or managing the business (beyond the wife's regular job description). A deal was quickly reached, they invested the $15k and we were off to the races.

The bad news is that this business never got off the ground. I invested money in moving the location to a larger, more visible spot in the community, upgraded equipment, hired better staff, etc. We made multiple, costly trips to the location several states away in an attempt to augment business (it was over 500 miles away)…all to no avail. When I finally was forced into a decision, I sold the business for $1 to another local businessperson who later decided to close it down completely. Over the course of time, I had both invested…and lost…over $40,000—not including the cost of trips, purchased supplies, etc.

Now because I am a good friend, I mailed a check to this couple for $5,000 of their initial $15,000 investment. Included with the check was a letter, explaining that I was mailing them this money, even though it was investment and I had no legal obligation to give them any of their money back. Very simply, I knew that this husband would relentlessly harass his wife and child over this for infinity…and I felt that they were such close friends that I couldn't bear to see that happen. As it turned out, I was more right than I knew!

As my son and I were returning from a holiday trip on Thanksgiving weekend of 2007, the sheriff pulled into my driveway. In his hand was service of a lawsuit. You guessed it…this greedy man was filing suit—convinced that I had money hiding somewhere that was rightfully his. I won't bore you with the details, because frankly they are too painful to have to reiterate, but this legal battle went on throughout the remainder of 2007 and most of 2008. I sat in court and had to watch as this spiteful man glared at me while telling the judge that I must have money somewhere…all while his wife looked down at her shoes (in shame?). When the final letter came in late September of 2008 advising me of a required pre-trial court date for a jury trial in State Court —the same month I had received the letter from my mortgage company advising of the impending foreclosure proceedings—I knew that it was the perfect storm. Bankruptcy would stop those proceedings as well. No thanks, Debbie & Jerry.

Yes, there was yet another lawsuit…this one far less personal. A business that I had sold about a year earlier required an official "subleasing" of the location to the new owner. The entire process was documented through the landlord, approving the new owner and extending the term of the lease. However, when the new owner decided to leave with no notice about 9 months into the new lease, the landlord decided to sue everyone within earshot to recoup their losses. Yes…the sheriff was back at my door. I was becoming paranoid every time I heard the sound of a car!

It was now mid October. How many more thumps on the head did God need to send me for me to take action? I once heard it said that when a person commits suicide, they don't chose it—it simply appears to them as their only option. Without being overdramatic, I would liken my situation to being pushed so far into one very small corner that the only way out was to throw up my hands and surrender. There was no figuring this out…no overtaking this hill like I had so many others in my life. The time to give up had clearly come.

In the end, I had to sell my precious little convertible (on the cover of this book) to raise enough money to file for bankruptcy because it was all I had left. That covered the down payment…then I had to write four checks dated the first of each month for the remainder of the payment to the attorney. While he was willing to work with me, the reason he had me write post-dated checks was very simple. If he deposited any of those checks on the check date and they didn't clear, he could take me to court for writing bad checks. Very clever….and very convincing. I knew I'd have to find a way to make good on those checks over the next four months.

So, just in case you think you are in a completely desperate situation, re-read this chapter! Everyone's situation…and their tolerance for handling it…is different. But here's the most important thing you need to take away from all of this --

I'M STILL STANDING!!!

CHAPTER 5

"Let it Be"

A Primer in Deciding What is Important

On Halloween 2008, I officially filed for bankruptcy (poetic, don't you think?). The gift that I gave myself was to put an end to all the harassing phone calls. Wow....the silence was golden! All those months of watching the phone ring 20-30 times a day were over!!! The process from filing to discharge of a Chapter 7 bankruptcy takes about 5 months on average...so I figured that I had some time to take a deep breath and figure things out. I had a brief moment of euphoria before the depression set in.

I paid my November car payment like usual, but the mail suddenly stopped from all creditors...secured and unsecured. A phone call to my attorney's office assured me that I wouldn't have to make any car payments during this period either. Now I felt like I had at least grabbed onto a tree and stopped the horrible downward slide I had been on for so long.

But let's review...I may have had few payments to make, but I still had absolutely NO income! The business had finally opened during the summer, but it appeared that the economy was on its own slide down the mountainside right behind me. Now bad

financial news was everywhere. Impending doom was advertised daily like a bad movie trailer! In September of 2008, gas shortages caused panic and long lines across the metro Atlanta area, creating the eerie atmosphere of a disaster movie in the making. It seemed like Armageddon was upon us. Everyone pulled back…including a group of investors we had been working with in the new business for several months. The bottom, it seemed, had fallen out everywhere.

In the wake of this sudden panic in the marketplace, I was filing for bankruptcy. It did seem to me that there was no light at the end of the tunnel. I thank God that I had my son. He was the only reason I was able to get myself out of bed on many of those days when the problems seemed completely insurmountable. He had to be driven to school…and he had to somehow finish growing up through all of this!

One evening in late November, I decided it was finally time for he and I to sit down and talk about our financial situation. Up to that point, I had told him very little…and he had asked no questions. While I have always loved to travel, we did so much less frequently and frugally over the past few years. He was…and is…not a spoiled child and is accustomed to hearing no, so his world had not changed too significantly. Or so I thought…

When we sat down that evening and I gave him the 14 year-old version of bankruptcy and foreclosure, he told me that he had known all along. As Dr. Phil says, kids are pretty darn smart…and he had ascertained quite some time ago that our situation had dramatically changed. Shame on me for not talking to him about this sooner. He knew that a move was imminent, saw that the house was up for sale, and had come to see it as a fresh start for us after all those years in the same house…what a positive spinner! But that night when I asked him if he had any questions for me, he said he had only one….would we have enough money to buy food. My heart shattered on the floor.

That night is the only time I can remember crying. I sat on the couch and cried for over two hours. How had I gone from a successful businessperson, financially stable and happy in my work to being completely broke with no clear solution in sight? I cried about all things I had lost. It seemed like the tears would never stop. I cried until I physically couldn't cry anymore.

I woke up the next morning with more resolve than ever. I knew it was time to start looking for a job. I guess that the dream of continued entrepreneurialism that I had held onto for so long needed to be shelved, at least for now. So I began my quest that very day working every angle that I could imagine to find employment. Now my single goal in life was to keep my son and I together…even if it meant living in our car.

It was now time for me to crawl out of my cocoon of silence and start connecting again. No one could help if they didn't know I needed help! Pride is another one of those useless emotions. So what if all those people I knew back then found out that I was broke now? There is nothing like kicking into pure survival mode to get yourself past a little remaining pride!

I began the process of getting in touch with people I hadn't spoken to in years. Remember, it had been almost 13 years since I had received a paycheck from anyone other my own companies, so some of my contacts had long ago moved on.

None of that stood in the way of me working every angle to re-enter the marketplace. I joined networking groups…I scoured the web…I sent out resumes, called recruiters. But remember…this was the end of 2008—NOT a great time to be on the market. November came and went…and NOTHING!!! December presented itself with even less prospects, as the holidays weighed heavily on everyone's mind in the emerging financial crisis. I truly started to panic!

So, in December of 2008, I went to what I had held as my plan B (or C or F!). I had long thought that if all else failed, I could return to teaching. My teaching certificates had long ago expired, but with the shortage of teachers they had experienced several years ago, the county in which I reside made the decision to pay substitute teachers a higher rate if they had a teaching certificate, even if it was expired. Resigning myself to this plan, I started asking questions, only to find that I needed to attend an orientation class before I could begin substituting. No so bad, until I discovered that the class was held only once every other month…and the last two classes had filled up within 30 minutes of being offered! Now even my plan F seemed to be out of my reach! It would be January before I could get into a class and early February before I received the required documentation to actually get on the list to be called as a substitute. We were certainly in uncharted waters.

So here I was…knowing that I would lose my house at some point in the near term…seemingly out of options to generate income…and responsible for raising a son to become the type of man who understands and shoulders his responsibilities. I worried about him throughout the process, but especially now, as he seemed completely unaffected by the ongoing deterioration of our financial life.

Right before Christmas, I decided that I would call on the help of a friend and pastoral minister that I have known for years through my church. He graciously offered to see us the very next day. On the way to the appointment, I stopped at the bank to deposit some cash that I had made from selling a few things. It seemed to be a long wait at the drive through, and finally someone bellowed out that I would have to come inside! Turns out that three of the four twenty-dollar bills that I had received in this transaction were counterfeit! In addition to being horrified and embarrassed, I now realized that a precious $60 that I thought I had was no longer. In the midst of me attempting to process that revelation, the teller told me that I had to step into the back. I was being questioned for passing counterfeit money!!!

So here's where I make a plug for local banking! Fortunately, I knew the branch manager of this particular institution fairly well. He came over after being informed about the situation and assured me that it would be fine, but that I would have to complete some Federal paperwork. They sat me down at his desk to complete the form that was supposed to be filled out by a bank officer. It was only then that I realized the seriousness of the situation! The form included questions like, "Is the person in front of you a suspect in the distribution of this counterfeit currency?" "Have the police been notified?" "Is an arrest eminent?" Oh my gosh!!! Needless to say, we were late for the appointment. But we did win the award for the most unique excuse for being late that this pastoral counselor had ever heard!

My gracious friend sat down and spoke to my son about what was happening. He asked him how he was doing. He inquired about school. He asked if he understood what was going on. He wondered if my son had any unanswered questions. My son very calmly told him about the night he had asked if we would have enough money for food. Then he said that he had seen his mother break down for the first time in his life.

It only took about 20 minutes for my friend to tell me that everything was alright. He said that he was so proud to see what a mature young man my son had grown into over the years...and that his reaction to what was happening was completely normal and well within what was reasonable to expect from someone of his age. He walked us out, telling me what a great job I had done of raising such a fine young man. Thanks Neal.

While we were standing in the parking lot chatting in this busy suburban area, two deer appeared out of nowhere. It took my breath away. Deer have always seemed to appear to me when something significant was about to happen, or when a shift was in the air, or when I simply needed assurance that everything was going to be all right. My son and I sat in the car and held each other for a few minutes before driving home.

That night I decided to go home for Christmas. Nothing was really different on the outside....but we were different on the inside. The mother/son bond was stronger than ever, and it

seemed like the right decision to be with family for Christmas. So
we did.

It was a long long drive....we made the 13 hour drive
without stopping. My son slept (probably from exhaustion!!), and it
really gave me time to process. I still had no job, no money,

impending bankruptcy and the loss of our family home...but it now

seemed to make more sense that ever that I get myself connected
to those important to me. I have a history of burrowing in when
things are bad. Not healthy. I had to get moving, get connected
and find a way to bring some money in.

CHAPTER 6

"Money, That's What I Want"

Find Money—Saving Money—Making Money

P.S. Nobody Wants Your Fur Coat!!

Truer words were never spoken. I remember back long ago when I had more money than I could spend. I remember saying things like "If a couple hundred bucks could make a significant difference to me, I'd really be in trouble." Yeah, now I was in trouble. $200 could almost make a car payment. Here I was with no job and no income, and I needed to get creative.

No T.A.R.P. money...but there is help

Use the resources available to you!

Much to my chagrin, I was in a desperate enough situation by early summer of 2008 that I literally was having trouble buying groceries. At the urging of a friend, (and I mean some serious urging!), I decided to go online and investigate the possibility of public assistance. Where do I begin telling you how horrifying this thought was!? Like most people, I thought that food stamps were mostly used by women with 14 kids by 14 different fathers living in a single-wide trailer. I was so resistant! Shame on me.

My friend continued to explain that I had paid taxes for all of my adult life, and it was my turn now. So after many conversations and lots of thought, I searched the web. Much to my surprise, today you can apply for food stamps on the web! I downloaded the form, completed it and faxed it in.

Within a week, I received a call from my local office requesting that I come in for a determination.

I showed up at the appointed time, sitting in the waiting room of a dingy little office with mostly Hispanic speaking people. This was going to be horrible!!

When it was finally my turn to get called back, I was greeted by a very pleasant middle-aged woman who looked like she had more work than she could handle. After a few minutes explaining my situation, she looked at me in horror and said that she was going to fill out the forms for emergency food assistance. Her concern was so sincere that it almost drove me to tears. "Do you have health insurance" was her next question. Since it had been several months since I had been able to pay those premiums, the answer, of course, was no! She pulled out more forms and started the process of applying for Medicaid assistance for both my son & I. By the time I left, I had a list of things to do and forms to fill out. Even though I was at the financial lowest point, I left being touched that someone actually cared that much about my situation. Within a few days I had a debit card that gave me a little over $300 a month for food. WOW!

The process of applying for and receiving help from the government is ongoing. Shortly after my first visit, I was summoned back to the office to meet with the child support division. Apparently (at least in my state!), if you apply for any type of government assistance where a child is involved, the non-custodial parent must be contributing. If they are not, as was in my case, you are sent to the child support division so that they may initiate a case against the non-custodial parent for support. No choice in the matter. All of these years, I had not made an issue of enforcing the custody/child support provision of our divorce case, as my ex-husband has always been self-employed. I assumed that a) finding him and b) getting him to actually pay anything would be next to impossible. But this time I didn't have a choice.

We went through the entire story again, and I had to compute exactly how much my ex-husband owed in child support. Even though I was awarded a very small monthly amount in the final divorce, take that amount x 12 months x 13 years…and it really adds up to something!

In the end, the caseworker wasn't very assuring…but it had to be done for us to qualify for Medicaid and non-emergency "food stamps". I submitted the paperwork and left without a thought.

Here's the interesting part…a few months later, I received a letter from the state in which my ex-husband now resides. Not only had they found him, but they had scheduled a court date!! Long story short…I didn't have to go to court, but made friends with the gal in the D.A.'s office….and they started levying his unemployment wages! Unbelievable as it sounds, he was currently on his own form of government assistance, and they handily garnished those payments to start making the required $77 a week payments that he was supposed to be making all along. Let me tell you, that was sent from heaven! I now at least had a little bit of money coming in on a regular basis! And to think that $77 a week really seemed like a lot! Boy, had things changed for me.

In the end, I received assistance for about 9 months during my bankruptcy process. This is not something I tell you with pride. However, I'm not sure how I would have made it without that help. My son now had health insurance through Medicaid that allowed him to play sports at his school, and we had money for groceries. All in all, this amounted to about an $877 benefit to me each month---$327 for groceries and $550 that I had been paying previously for health insurance premiums. THAT is a LOT of money!!

My approval letter for food stamps also gave me all I needed to get my son on the free lunch program at his school. Again, not really proud—but necessary. He never knew, and I saved another $50 or so a month on food while he was at school. Every little bit helps!

Why Welfare is Self-Perpetuating:

So, you wonder why welfare seems to be generational? Let's take a quick look. I was advised that once my gross monthly income (in my state for a family of 2) reached $1,579, I had to report the change immediately to my caseworker. This could mean the end of my benefits. Okay, so let's do the math. If my gross income reached that amount, I would be bringing home about $1,340 a month. If I were lucky enough to get a job, I would have the additional cost of gas & car maintenance for transportation to get to and from work. Let's estimate that CONSERVATIVELY at about $150 a month. If my son were 4 or 5 years younger, I would have to pay for childcare. Since I've been there, let's say that cost is about $172 (more if your child is younger and not in school yet!).

So…making slightly more than $300 a week net, I would lose over $927 in benefits ($327 for groceries, $50 in school lunch assistance, $550 in health insurance premiums for my son & I). Then I would have those additional expenses, conservatively totaling approximately $322 per month. My net gain from working would be about $91 a month—and that's without considering other expenses associated with working (dry cleaning, lunches out, etc.) No wonder people stay on welfare.

Here are the facts. The Federal Income Level Chart below lists the amount of money by household size that can be considered for government assistance. Do the math.

FEDERAL INCOME CHART					
For School Year 2009-2010					
Household size	Yearly	Monthly	Twice Per Month	Every Two Weeks	Weekly
1	20,036	1,670	835	771	386
2	26,955	2,247	1,124	1,037	519
3	33,874	2,823	1,412	1,303	652
4	40,793	3,400	1,700	1,569	785
5	47,712	3,976	1,988	1,836	918
6	54,631	4,553	2,277	2,102	1,051
7	61,550	5,130	2,565	2,368	1,184
8	68,469	5,706	2,853	2,634	1,317
Each additional person:	+6,919	+577	+289	+267	+134

Do know that they check everything. On one of the many visits that I had to make to the office for verification, the caseworker noticed that I had my nails done. Yup, I was now in a position where I had to defend spending $27 every two months to get my nails done. I was out doing everything I could to get a job...and it seemed to me to be an expense that I had to find money for. She wasn't so convinced. Everything in my life was up for questioning.

By the way, if you are lucky enough NOT to qualify for Medicaid, but still can't afford insurance for your kids, most states have a state funded insurance program for low-income families. So even if you are working, but are well on your way to being broke, I would encourage you to find out if your state has one! Georgia has PeachCare for kids...just do a Google search for your state to see if you can qualify. The monthly payments are VERY reasonable.

Don't hesitate to look for other assistance in your area. In my state, there is an organization called The Ninth District...not really sure who they are, but what they do is provide information on organizations that can help you in your area. United Way serves as a clearinghouse for places in and around your community that can help you with food, utility assistance and other short term needs. In many areas, you can simply dial 211 to reach your local United Way agency. I was referred to one organization that was able to assist me with food and another that helped me with a utility bill that I just couldn't scrape the money together for. You might also ask your church...although for me, that was the toughest. (There's that pride thing again!)

There are also lots of food banks popping up all over the place. These are usually based out of churches, but anyone can come and purchase about $80 worth of food for about $30. Unlike applying for food stamps or receiving assistance from United Way funded agencies, all you have to do is show up and say you need help. Call a few local churches in your area to see if there is something similar to this in your area.

Now that I had taken care of some basics, I figured it was time to take a hard look around to see how I could either reduce my living costs or bring in some money…or both! I took several steps that seem obvious now…and really saved me! Hopefully you will find the same if you look at a few of these opportunities in your own situation.

I've broken this down into four categories:

<u>Finding Money</u>, <u>Saving Money</u>,

<u>Making Money</u> & <u>Finding Work</u>.

The key here is that you have to do all 4 of these at once! So get busy…your financial life depends on it!

FINDING MONEY

<u>Insurance:</u>

Check out ALL your insurance policies—can you reduce your car insurance by raising your deductible? Might not be your first choice in good times, but when things are tough, a higher deductible can make a big difference in your premium. I went from a $500 deductible to a $2,000 deductible…and paid a lot more attention while I was driving! But it saved me over $25 a month…a lot over time! I also had an umbrella policy that had been important when I owned a business, but completely irrelevant now…nothing for anyone to get if they sued me at this point?! So I cancelled that and saved another $12 per month on my insurance bill.

Let me say that the one insurance policy I was sure to keep (besides car insurance!) was my life insurance policy. As a single mom, I needed to be sure that if anything did happen to me, there would be some money for my son. So in spite of the fact that I was soooo broke, I've never missed a payment.

<u>Utilities:</u>

*Review ALL of your utility bills to see where there might be opportunities to save money. Even if the savings is small, it all adds up! And at this point, a few dollars each month was really significant! Make sure that you compare 'apples to apples', so you won't get locked into a service that really doesn't save you money. And look around for offers! I switched my natural gas service and got a great introductory rate that lasted for several months AND a rebate check for $75!

*I knew I still needed the Internet, but as fast as this technology was moving, I figured there must be some better deals out there. In the end, I switched my Internet provider and got a bundle rate, which decreased my overall phone/Internet bill by about $40 a month…and another rebate check—this time for $175!!! Again, A BIG DEAL!!!

*TV or not TV. I am not one of those people that can survive without television…sorry. But I did switch my provider and got another low, intro rate that helped me to keep at least basic cable. Times are tough and deals are out there. Look…I mean REALLY LOOK at what you are paying for things…and start negotiating!

Paper money:

*Any old stocks or bonds lying around? Believe it or not, I had an old stock certificate in with my legal documents that I had completely forgotten about! In the end, it was about $400 worth of found money, which made my car payment and more that month! I had to set up a brokerage account with my local bank to transact the sale, but the $35 that cost me was well worth it!

I wish I would have known then about Zecco Trading (www.Zeccotrading.com). This is an online service with little to no customer service, but you can trade for as little as FREE – with some stipulations…or $4.50 per trade! Too late for me, unless I get rich again and decide to try some day trading!

*Savings bonds, anyone? Okay, so I'm not that great of a mom. My son had received several savings bonds over the years from my sister, a gift that she thoughtfully made each year on his birthday. I'm not proud, but at one point, this was the only currency available to me. Yup, I cashed 'em in.

If you have any Series E savings bonds lying around, you can determine their current worth   by going to the Treasury's Savings Bond Calculator (www.treasurydirect.gov/BC/SBCPrice). If your bonds were purchased from 1974 forward, you will be able to plug in the serial number of your bond and get the current cash-in value. Look for the site's Treasury Hunt tool. If you have bonds purchased prior to 1974, you'll have to write the Bureau of Public Debt, P.O. Box 7012, Parkersburg, WV 26106-7012. Include as much information as you can, including serial #s, bondholder's name and address at the time of purchase, etc. By the way, bonds owned by the deceased can still be cashed by their heirs.

Negotiate Everything:

As I mentioned earlier, my original plan was to keep my 2007 Chevy that I was making payments on. However, prior to bankruptcy filing, those payments were getting harder and harder to make. So I called. Immediately, they offered me the opportunity to skip a payment, then make several half-payments over the next few months. It made a huge difference at a time when money was so tight I can't even describe it.

SAVING MONEY

I can see clearly now:

In spite of the fact that I was broke, my son still needed new glasses. I found this GREAT website where I purchased glasses for him for $8.00! YES, I said $8.00!!! They are made in Russia or something, but the quality is the same as you'd get anywhere! It takes a little longer, but hey, it's $8.00!! www.zennioptical.com

Have some fun!

We have a pretty cool comedy club near me that has been around forever called The Punchline. I'm on their weekly e-mail list, and they often hide little surprise incentives for those of us paying attention! Recently, one of the e-mails had a little line at the bottom that said something like "If you've read this far, you deserve something free—call us to get a buy one/get one free ticket!!!

You know I did…so my friend and I split the cost of a $25 admission! Here's the best part! They do a drawing at each show if you drop your business card in the bowl on the way in. Turns out I was the big winner that night! I won a $25 gift certificate! I actually MADE MONEY on the trip!!! Recently, they've even been offering FREE shows on certain Wednesday, Thursday & Sunday nights! Go now, go often! It pays to pay attention!!!

Sign Up!

And speaking of e-mails…sign up for just about everything you think you are interested in!!!

I have gotten some MONSTER deals on everything from restaurants to baseball tickets to hotels! If you are on their mailing lists, you'll be the first to take advantage of some great great deals! (or simply pass those travel deals on to your friends who can afford to travel ☹)

Twitter away!

Are you on it!? You should be! Twitter is a great way to stay up to date and connected with what's going on! If you find the accounts you're interested in, you simply hit "follow" when you land on their page. (Really, it's simple! I'm not a techie and I figured it out!!!). I've not only saved money on restaurants, etc., but get some great inside tips on job openings in my area 'cause I found a site that is called...wait for it...Georgia Jobs! Get on it!

Do it yourself:

I have two Yorkshire Terriers (or should I say Terriors!). I have always tried to keep them groomed and clean, but never thought that I would be capable of cutting their hair (yes...Yorkies have HAIR and not FUR!). Anyway, I decided to see how I would do. So I took one of the outside with my sharpest scissors and

voila! It might not be exactly the same as the groomer's cut, but I saved myself $40!!!!!!!! And that is PER DOG!!! I have even gotten one of the new "as seen on T.V." grinders to help me trim their nails without all the drama....

Buying gas?

Then you should care how much it costs!! Every little bit helps...I joined a local grocery store's loyalty program and now regularly save .03 cents per gallon on every fill up! Even better, once I reach $100 in grocery spending at their stores, I get a bonus .10 cents per gallon off! That's a lot!! You can also go to sites like Gas Buddy (www.GasBuddy.com) to find the cheapest gas today by zip code!

Buy in bulk:

And speaking of groceries, there's a lot to be said about buying in bulk, but only if you will really use it. Since it is just my son and I, the items I buy a lot of are always ones that can be frozen. For that reason, I purchased a freezer that I've kept in the garage for years. That way, when I find frozen dinners for .78 cents each, I can stock up! Comes in really handy now that I have a teenage boy in the house!

Thrift Stores:

I now know the beauty of these gems. I'm not a big fan of consignment stores...they always seem to smell like old clothes and dead people. But thrift stores, like the ones operated by

Goodwill and other localized charities have some real gems! These are the places where (often wealthy) people donate things that they don't need/feel guilty about having/want out of the house/need a tax deduction for. I have purchased everything from Hart Marx wool suit for my son ($12) to a set of golf clubs, bag and all ($7) to Polo shirts ($3)...and much more! You are helping people by funding these organizations...and certainly helping yourself by finding such deals! GO!

Coupons anyone?:

I have always clipped coupons. I know that popular new age thinking tells you that by clipping coupons you are telling the universe that you don't believe in its abundance and thereby create negative energy. Baloney. Clip away.

In addition to your local Sunday paper (which costs $2.00 and often nets you hundreds of dollars worth of coupons!), you should also sign up for the mailing list of anybody and everybody that you can think of doing business with. Local grocery stores now e-mail out weekly coupons. Restaurants are discounting heavily with special promotions due to the current economic conditions. Some will even mail you special discounts for your birthday! Even luxury hotels are offering special packages that save hundreds…so this is not just for those of us who are circling the drain financially!

You should also sign up for store e-mail lists. You'll often get advance notice of sales and additional coupons for $$s off. Seek out locations that have special incentives for signing up. National drug store chains (like CVS) have their own loyalty programs that net you something free or $5 off a purchase of $10 fairly frequently!

Don't forget about the big sites online. Here are a few you should check out, just so you are in the know! You'll be amazed at the things you can get deals on! These can come and go….Google "coupons" for your city to get a really current list!

- www.CouponCraze.com

- www.CouponMom.com

- www.GoGoShopper.com

- www.CouponCabin.com

- www.RetailMeNot.com

- www.Dealio.com

- www.MommySavesBig.com

- www.HalfOffDepot.com

- www.Groupon.com (you can even get deals on dance classes here!!!)

Again…stay up to date on daily deals and the most current info on blogs…my new favorite is called "Hey, it's free!" (www.heyitsfree.net). I've even gotten free laundry detergent!!

Don't forget to sprinkle in some treats!

Even though I was beyond broke, I took it as a personal challenge to see if I could still maneuver a way to have a little fun. One day, I received a solicitation in the mail for a timeshare in Florida. Since Florida is within driving distance for us, I read it through carefully. The only obligation was to sit through a timeshare presentation for 90 minutes and bring a credit card (which was my debit card by this point!). In exchange, we would get three nights in a hotel, a $75 gas card and a $50 dining certificate…all for only $65! We were able to take a quick vacation that cost almost nothing—and really changed my perspective, at least for a few days!

Travel deals really abound right now. Some of the best places to look for hotel deals are listed below:

Hotwire.com (www.Hotwire.com)

Priceline.com (www.Priceline.com)

(Be sure to check www.BiddingforTravel.com before you bid to see what prices others have been getting!)

Quikbook.com (www.Quikbook.com)

LastMinute.com (www.LastMinute.com)

LuxuryLink.com (www.LuxuryLink.com)

(Yes…you CAN get deals on luxury these days!)

ALWAYS check on what people are saying before you book—sites like TripAdvisor (www.TripAdvisor.com) are great at giving you real person accounts of places that can sound great on the company website!

Yapta.com is another great source. This site is an aggregator that tells you the lowest price for flights, hotels, cars and other travel deals. Other aggregators include Mobissimo (www.Mobissimo.com) and SideStep (www.SideStep.com). Some of these sites have predictor software that will track your desired flight/destination and e-mail you when prices go up or down. Yapta even shows you a chart that graphically tells you when you should wait, buy or not buy. Amazing stuff!

Then, just to be sure you are happy with your seat on the plane, check out Seatguru (www.SeatGuru.com). You'll be able to see the layout of the flight you're on and locate the exact seat number that's ideal for you! Remember that many airlines are now charging a fee for certain seat selections, but it makes sense to check it out! Then, to be sure the room in your hotel has the best view or isn't over the kitchen, check out Trip Kick (www.TripKick.com). If your hotel is in their data base, you can get specific recommendations on exactly which room you should pick. Very cool!

Eating out is a luxury that we had to virtually eliminate. However, I did find Restaurant.com, where you can buy greatly discounted coupons for local restaurants. I was able to buy $10 gift certificates for as low as 80 cents each! YES...I said eighty cents!!! With that, we could go to a restaurant and have dinner for about $10! Not something we did often, but it was certainly a wonderful treat when some unexpected money came in and we needed a boost! Go to their website (www.Restaurant.com) and sign up to be on their e-mail list for the best discounts! I do this EVERY time we are going somewhere....you can really eat on the cheap when you are traveling to those great hotel deals you'll find!

MAKING MONEY

For the first time ever, I found that being a collector had big benefits. Most days I spent an hour or so around the house taking pictures of stuff that now meant nothing to me and listing it on CRAIG'S LIST. Some weeks I made nothing…other weeks I made three or four hundred dollars!! I had stuff sitting around from my son's youth, from former business projects, and just plain stuff that I didn't want anymore! So I became an expert at writing catchy headlines for listings on Craig's List. You can also list on Amazon and E-Bay…but Craig's List has one huge advantage—IT'S FREE!!!! (www.CraigsList.com)

I managed to sell everything you can imagine here. I sold old birdcages (and reconnected with my son's first grade teacher!!). I sold a church pew that was sitting in my basement. I sold a bunch of old CDs and albums that had been gathering dust since the 70's. (Don't get too excited…they weren't worth that much!)

Word of caution…NO ONE WANTS YOUR FUR COAT! Anything of value is really a tough sell right now! People are looking for the basics. You can sell a toaster, but you might have a tough time selling an old engagement ring. Times are tough…play to the audience and you won't waste your time!

Here's another side benefit. Craig's List forces you to get out and meet people! Unlike the anonymous shipping protocol on E-Bay and others, when someone wants your stuff from Craig's List, you eventually have to meet them somewhere to make the exchange. I met some of the nicest people in parking lots and gas stations selling things from Craig's List. Kind of restores your faith in people!

Ever had a GARAGE SALE? No time is better for than then when you know you're moving! I ended up having two garage sales and selling the darndest stuff...and made over $500 both times!

FLEA MARKETS are great places to go if you have a lot of one category of stuff. One very cold Sunday in December, my son and I packed the car with all of my excess luggage and handbags and drove about an hour and a half away to set up shop in an outdoor flea market. People come from all across the state to wander these isles...some stuff is new, some not. We got a table/space for only $25, and ended up selling a lot of pieces that were probably headed for the garbage dump...and made about $200! Who woulda' thought it?

I'm sure you've heard the ads that now proliferate for SELLING GOLD & JEWELRY. Let me just tell you one this...no one wants your jewelry either. They will pay for gold—broken, tangled…it doesn't matter. They weigh it and pay you the going rate. I ended up doing this several times…first in a department store who was having an "antique road show" type of 2-day event, then at a hotel ballroom sale. Each time I came away with more than I expected. If you have something that is heavy with gold that has no sentimental value to you, go for it!

Can you imagine getting PAID TO DRIVE YOUR CAR??? You may have heard of this and thought it was a scam…and there may well be some scams out there! There are a couple of legit companies that I know of that will pay you to "wrap" your car, provided you meet their current needs based on where you live, the location of your commute, whether or not you have children, logged number of miles per month, etc. This form of advertising has actually been around for about 10 years, and has morphed from the companies leasing the cars for you to drive to the now more cost effective method of writing you a check & wrapping your car! Check out Free Car Media (www.FreeCarMedia.com) and Driven Media (www.DrivenMediaOnline.com) and sign up so your name is in their company's databases. DON'T pay to sign up for any service! Simply answer the questionnaire, submit…and see if you get picked!! Don't expect this to be a quick fix…but it could net you as much as $900 if you are selected!

But speaking of quick fixes…search your area for legitimate focus groups. I have responded to a few of these ads and actually was selected to test drive a car and give feedback. It took about 2 hours, but I made $50! It had been a while since I made $25 an hour!

Ever thought of clinical trials? I know it may seem bizarre, but you can make some real money and/or do some cool things! After the fact I found out about one study on the effects of jet lag. (Okay, I really did see it in time, but I was skeptical, so I didn't respond...duh!). The group that was selected went on several back to back over seas flights! Now that would have been cool! I don't know what that study paid, but the adventure would have been worth it to someone like me who loves to travel!

I did find a clinical trial where I did respond and I was accepted! In exchange for taking a new drug and agreeing to have my vital signs monitored, I found myself walking out of the first visit with $100 in cash in my pocket! Some of these studies can go on for week...or months! Check out Craigslist and other local listings to find something in your area!

Ever read a blog? Believe it or not, there's money in those things! If people are interested in what you are saying, you may find yourself in a position to make money by creating your own blogging site! And it's done while you sleep! Seriously, by allowing advertisers on your site, you can make what is called a "passive" income while you are out doing other thing! The best part is that you don't have to go out and look for those advertisers...aggregators like Google Ads and others will find advertisers for you and place them on your site!

Advertisers come in two major categories. There are PPC (pay per click) models and click through models (that pay you when someone follows a link and then makes a purchase) are the two ways you can gain revenue. Of course, the amount of traffic your site has is a definite determiner in how much you will make...but, hey, if a site like People of WalMart (www.PeopleofWalmart.com) can make money...so can you!!!

FINDING WORK

As I said earlier, I was on a CONSTANT job search, I knew that I had to look everywhere and be aggressive. I joined several networking groups (NOT my favorite thing, but necessary). There is a great website where you can get business cards for free. It's Vista Print (www.VistaPrint.com). I was able to go to networking groups with something other than a slip of paper with my phone number on it! I needed every edge I could get!

After scouring the "help wanted" ads and Craig's List, I eventually drew the conclusion that there were several bookkeeping/"help me get organized" kind of jobs out there...so I threw a website together and formed a business to professionally approach those openings. Vista Print got me a very cheap website, business cards and all I needed to make it look like I had been at it for years… Did I mention that I LOVE them!

Remember, if you are self-employed, you can't get fired! Instead of living in fear of "the man" (or woman!), maybe it's time you took your fate into your own hands. What do you like to do? What are the kinds of things you find yourself drawn to? Do you see a need somewhere in there? I have a small sign in my office that goes something like this, "Where your passion meets the needs of the world…there you shall make your fortune". Pretty cool when you think of it that way!

If you take a close look at current trends, you'll see that the 'baby boomer' generation is moving through the world like a rat down a snake's body (that's an uplifting analogy, isn't it?). Seriously, we as a group/generation use up more of the world's resources than any other, especially in the U.S. What are some of the needs/wants of baby boomers? That's easy! None of us wants to grow old, and if we do, we want to be in our own homes to do it.   Therapeutic therapies like massage and skin care are big…"active adult" homes and activities are growing as a segment every year. And if you have an aging parent, you'll understand the rapid rise of in-home senior care services. You could start your own or buy a franchise!

If you are so inclined, check out your local S.C.O.R.E. office (Service Corp. of Retired Executives) in your area. Here you can get free mentoring from someone who's been there…and get a real leg up! There are also sites on the web that can help you find or clarify your passion…check around!

Do you like to write? Consider yourself a budding author? Check out sites like Media Bistro (www.mediabistro.com), Helium (www.Helium.com) and Write Jobs (www.WriteJobs.com). Looking for project work? Look at Sologig (www.Sologig.com). Think you want to teach? Check out sites like www.Tutor.com are looking for individuals that are college educated (generally) who have specific specialties listed on their websites.

Think you are an expert on something? Anything? Even if the expertise is just about YOU…you can create a blog! Why not! As I said earlier, there are many ways to monetize blogs these days. Check out Google Ads and others or do a google search on "affiliate marketing" to find sites that could potentially bring revenue to your daily rumblings… Guest blogging or becoming a resident blogger for another site could actually become a real job!

I have heard that Donald Trump believes that the best way for anyone to become wealthy today is to become a part of an MLM (multi-level marketing) or direct selling business. No, these are not pyramid schemes—I'm talking about the legitimate businesses where you have a very low initial investment and your payout is entirely dependent upon your efforts. This business model allows you to make unlimited money if you're willing to do the work.

Some businesses you might want to take a look at range from makeup (Mary Kay/Avon) to health care coverage (Aflac), StreamEnergy (**send me an e-mail...I'm actually doing this one!!!**), nutritional supplemnts (Shakelee), home décor (Southern Living)...the list is endless! One thing is for sure—you will never be able to start a business with less money!!

Find a "real" job:

For me, the search for that perfect job has been never ending. I troll the Craig's List ads, have joined Linked In and subscribe to several online job search engines. Other than the obvious ones (www.CareerTrack.com, www.CareerBuilder.com), sign yourself up with some of the bigger aggregators. Sites like American Jobs (www.AmericanJobs.com), Work in Retirement (www.RetirementJobs.com), Indeed (www.Indeed.com), Beyond (www.Beyond.com) and others troll the web to bring you relevant jobs if you take the time to set up your search criteria. Well worth doing and will save you some time so you don't just sit in front of your computer all day!!!

Keeping Track:

Want to check your credit score for free? DO NOT go to freecreditreport.com! These guys are scammers. AnnualCreditReport.com will give you access to each of your three credit reports once per year. Even better, sites like CreditKarma (www.CreditKarma.com) and Quizzle (www.Quizzle.com) will even give you your credit SCORE for free! Even better! And once you sign up, Credit Karma will even send you reminders telling you how long it's been since you've checked your score. This is a great way to stay focused on keeping this number moving in the right direction.

CHAPTER 7

"Get by with a little help from my friends"

Need I Say More?

The note below was sent by my dear friend who enclosed a check for $500, just when I thought I wasn't going to be able to keep the lights on that month.

This is my gift to you. I have faith that once again you will overcome difficult times

Love + blessings

Donna

Thanks, Donna...

In April of 2008, when things really bottomed out and I stopped paying everything, I had one very difficult phone call to make. A dear friend of mine who works as Executive V.P. of a local bank had made a loan to my business about a year earlier that I was now no longer able to repay. This was the notification that I dreaded the most. Not only had our sons been best friends since the second grade, but this man had previously invested in my business and was someone that I considered to be a close personal friend. I don't know if it was the pain of having to tell him that I was defaulting on the loan or the shame of having to admit that I'd failed…but I delayed making this phone call as long as I could.

When the time came that the payment was going to be late, I finally worked up the courage to call him. I explained that I wouldn't be making the payment that month and why, and then I told him the whole story. His reaction could have taken many forms…anger, resentment, you name it—I was prepared for the worst.

But here's what he did. He asked me to get in the car and drive to his office so he could take me out to lunch. He told me how he had been watching the signs of the economic melt down and that this was only the beginning (it was early in 2008, remember...the worst hadn't happened yet). He assured me that in years to come, having to report that I had filed for bankruptcy

during this time of economic disaster would be greeted with barely a stare by most. He asked what he could do to help. How could I have ever envisioned a more gracious response...or a better friend? Thanks Gary.

"Home" is the Chicago area. Even though I haven't lived there for 20 years, I still think of it that way. My sister and her husband live there...and her only daughter, my niece, who was the closest thing I had to a child until I had my own...she and her husband and two kids are there too (I love you, Jenny). Even the friends who were the first people to "meet" my son in the hospital the day after he was born in New Hampshire now live outside of Chicago. And don't forget all my childhood and early adult friends—I still go to my class reunions every five years! You see, I grew up in a small farming community outside Chicago with only 54 kids in my graduating class. While I'm one of the few who moved away, many of us still keep in regular communication and see each other on occasion.   So you see the ties are deep and wide.

Of course, I didn't have any money to go home for Christmas in 2008. And we had NEVER spent a Christmas morning away from home since my son was born—I always thought it was important for Santa to come to our house. But this year was different in so many ways...and being with family seemed like the right thing to do. That strong need to be connected was what was keeping me hanging on. I knew I couldn't afford to buy plane tickets, but I figured we could drive…although I wasn't even sure where I would get the money to do that!

Two days before we left, a very dear friend of mine called to say she was coming over. Odd. She is not one of those "impromptu" friends that just drop over…and she didn't just stop over unless she was dropping something off. But okay.

A few minutes later, she was at my door. Acting a bit nervous, she came in and sat down, making small talk about Christmas, asking how we were doing, etc. And she kept looking towards the front door. Within a few minutes, another dear friend (and next door neighbor) rang the bell. They both glanced nervously at each other. Now I thought I was the subject of an intervention….

Suddenly, the first friend to arrive stood up and told me she had something to say…and that I shouldn't interrupt her or she would never get through it. She proceeded to tell me that a lot of people loved and cared about my son and I. Knowing me, she knew that I wasn't about to ask anyone for help (Shame on me!). But she also knew exactly the situation I was in and decided that she was going to help whether I liked it or not. These two wonderful friends then handed me several envelopes—envelopes that contained gift cards and cash...LOTS of cash.

There were gift cards for restaurants, sporting goods stores, Wal*Mart, bookstores...you name it. In the end, there was almost $1,700 in cash and gift cards.

By now, we were all sobbing. They told me that they had gathered all this from friends who cared about us, wanted to help and wanted my son to have a Christmas. I was completely overwhelmed. All those years of being on the other side—adopting families for Christmas, serving holiday dinners to the homeless—never in a million years did I think I would be on the other side of that equation. And now, just when things seemed as out of my control and without hope as I could imagine, these wonderful people emerged with the gift of friendship. This was undoubtedly the best Christmas gift I had ever received. And I don't mean the money. Thanks Dottie & Nancy.

For the past several years, I have led the charge of missions at my church. While at first it was just the obligatory committee commitment, my passion quickly grew. Over time, we have expanded our church's involvement with local missions and a $7,500 annual budget to both local and global initiatives with an annual budget over $120,000. I have been blessed to participate in trips to Indian Reservations in Montana to boat trips down the Amazon…and many places in between.

What has all of that taught me? Well, many things. First, that we live in a country where abundance is considered the norm. Where five bedrooms and three baths is average…and outdoor plumbing is a thing from old movies and grandparent's tales. It has also put many things into perspective for me. In our society, results must be instantaneous and down time is considered a bad thing. But let me tell you this…there is nothing like connecting with someone over a campfire on the shore of The Amazon. You can't match the feeling of digging a latrine for a small church in a town where outhouses are considered luxuries. And nothing can top the feeling of telling a group of small children about the God who loves them…or top the love that you feel when presenting them with the first Polaroid pictures they have ever seen of themselves. The more you strip away, the more real it gets.

In many ways, those lessons were serving me well now. While I was in the worst shape of life financially, my heart was overwhelmed by the friendship and love being displayed to me by those I held dear. The gift if friendship I received that Christmas overshadowed any gift I had ever received…and there had been some whoppers! Like the Beatles have said for years…*"All you need is love…."*

CHAPTER 8

"The Long & Winding Road"

"The Legal Process—Timeline to Legally Going Broke"

So, here is the part of the book with the nitty gritty. These are the hard facts about what happens when, what to expect and how to act or react to what is happening. I'll say again that I am NOT an attorney, but this is the timing of my journey to brokenness...and what I learned in the process. May it help you as you pass through those gates and on to the rest of your life.

If you've gotten this far in the book, you know that I feared bankruptcy with all that was in me. I'm not sure if it was old psychological baggage or fear of the unknown...I just know that I had been keeping many balls in the air for a very long time in hopes of staving it off. For me, bankruptcy became the right (and only clear) answer. Your situation may be different and your circumstances your own...and you may reach a very different conclusion. But for what it's worth, here's how I got here.

Over the few years that my businesses were not doing well, I continued to try to maintain status quo. Fear of change? Don't think so...doesn't seem like me....but I wasn't really sure what else I would do. And you see, that eternal optimist thing kept getting in the way. I always thought things would get better. So when I borrowed money against the equity of my house, I didn't think of it as solving a debt problem with more debt. I thought I was simply putting money from one investment into another. Hmmm...maybe once. Doing it the second time with an almost double-digit interest rate should have woken me up...but by then, I was in it with both feet and then some.

As a person who had managed several multi-million dollar businesses with great acumen, strategy had been replaced by a very narrow vision of surviving. The credit card balances began to creep up. My house payment became beyond unreasonable. My entire world was boiled down to waking up, checking bank balances and transferring the necessary funds to cover that day's bills. I couldn't leave home overnight because I needed to be there to check bank balances every morning and pay the credit cards that were due that day. While I was never late, most all of my cards were maxed out. Soon credit card companies began raising the minimum payments to a percentage of the total instead of the previous set dollar amount. Then interest rates soared.

Some of my cards were as high as 36.99%!! But I still continued to pay the minimums without fail.

Had someone sat me down and forced me to take a strategic look at my situation, bankruptcy would most certainly have been a discussion at least 18 months sooner than I began entertaining it. However, because I didn't understand the process, I feared even asking the question. I knew that if I sold my business, I would be left with a certain amount of money to live off of while attempting to get my new business off the ground. Many months earlier, an attorney told me during a phone conversation that the courts would not look favorably at any lump sum sitting in the bank, so I convinced myself that I would sell my business and live off the proceeds...and yes, stave off bankruptcy in the process.

As I said earlier, that plan worked for a short while until one of the loans that I held on a business I had sold defaulted. Now I had absolutely NO income, even though I was working more than full time trying to get another business off the ground. The cash reserves that I had were dwindling fast. There was no listing the pluses and minuses of this situation—I was forced into my first dramatic step, credit counseling.

As Dr. Phil likes to say "How's that workin' out for ya' so far??" Within one month of going through the credit counseling service, my credit was shot. The process of getting approved by all the vendors for the program caused delays that made almost every payment late. My closely guarded credit score of 625 dove more than 100 points almost immediately.

I will say that this whole thing did serve to completely get my WHOLE attention. For the first time in a very long time, I sat down and saw the situation for what it was. As I looked at the credit counseling agreement I had embarked on, I was going to make payments of over $3,600 every month for five years...yes, FIVE YEARS! Forget the obvious question about where that money was going to come from...I finally took the helicopter view and saw clearly that I would struggle for five years to make these payments and still be in the credit "dog house" for the entire period. You see, most of your creditors will report that you are in a credit counseling repayment program, so no company would be likely to extend you any other credit for that entire period. Bankruptcy suddenly seemed like something to consider...after all, the affects last only 7 to 10 years and I wouldn't be struggling to repay a debt that I was unlikely to be able to cover each month.

But what did it all mean? Did it mean that I would have to sell my clothes and live in the car? I didn't know! So I set out to educate myself on the process. I briefly gave an overview of both Chapter 7 and Chapter 13, as I understand them, in an earlier part of this book. But here's the bottom line. Chapter 13 is something you do if you have a job (or some sort of regular income) and have debts that are more than 50% of that income. In other words, if it is highly unlikely that you will be capable of repaying the debt in a reasonable amount of time given your current situation, Chapter 13 provides a legal way for you to settle those debts and be able to breathe again.

As one attorney friend explained to me, bankruptcy is not designed to keep you from making a living. Since debtor's prisons no longer exist, bankruptcy is not designed to be a punitive process. Maybe that's why so many people take advantage of it? In any case, it has been created to offer a "fresh start"—a way to reset the start button and keep you from getting ulcers over the debt that you are carrying.

Since I did not hold a regular job, but was in the process of starting a business, I had a whole other set of fears. What if my business became successful in the short term? Could the courts assess that value and take a portion of it? Or would they consider the business an asset and take it in the sale? Not only was I worried about this; I had a business partner who had every reason to be just as concerned as I was about learning the answers to those questions. This required looking at the situation from a couple of different angles.

First, if you file for Chapter 13 reorganization, you will be under court supervision for the period of the repayment plan. Any sales or purchases of a major kind (cars, houses, etc.) will be under the direction and at the discretion of the trustee. In other words, if you are in a five-year repayment plan and in year three or four your business starts doing very well, the court may very well accelerate your repayment plan. Should you decide that you need a new car, that issue must be taken up with the court as well. As it was described to me, you would be on a very short leash. Even sales of existing assets must be discussed with and approved by the court. Not really a great fit for a free thinker such as myself!

Here's one interesting tidbit that was given to my several attorney friends--the lottery ticket example. If you file for bankruptcy today and win the lottery tomorrow, those winnings are exempt from the bankruptcy proceedings! In other words, if you have income that could not have been predicted prior to the date of the bankruptcy filing, it cannot be considered as a part of the bankruptcy. Pretty cool! However, the key there is predictability. You can't realistically predict that you will win the lottery (desperately hope, but not predict!)

If you own a business prior to the filing that later becomes successful, the discussion of predictability takes a different turn. If the business that I was starting now became successful later, it could well be considered in the long term of the bankruptcy proceedings. And technically the trustee could decide that it was worth something and force a sale. Big lesson relearned...only go into ventures of any kind with people you know and TRUST! Why do I mention this now? In short, if my business partner were the least bit scrupulous, she could have gone to the trustee and forced a sale of my 50% holdings—leaving her with the entire business and me with whatever amount she would put forth to the trustee. Good thing I only hang out with friends! Thanks Logan.

So again, my clear & only choice was to file Chapter 7. After all the bad information and lousy trips to "bankruptcy mill" offices, I found myself in front of a credible and reputable attorney in May of 2008. I mustered up the $250 for the initial visit. (And that wasn't easy!!!). After that first fateful meeting, he made it crystal clear that this was my only viable choice. But now for the timing—I could file now and make the water torture of relentless phone calls stop. But that would also accelerate the timing on the foreclosure of my house. I was only one month behind at this point, and had not yet received any threatening letters or phone calls from my mortgage company. And then there was the obvious—I didn't have the necessary funds! Minor detail, but at this point, I could not afford to file bankruptcy! What a hoot!

I got the best piece of advice I had received in my attorney's office that day. If I waited until foreclosure was eminent, I could file for bankruptcy as late as THE DAY BEFORE my house was to be auctioned on the courthouse steps and still stave off that bankruptcy sale!!! Wow! As you may have guessed, I somewhat enjoy living a bit on the edge, and this was the greatest game of chicken I had ever played! While I would have to live with several more months of annoying creditor phone calls, I would be able to stay in my house until this scenario play itself out! Not only was I up for that game…I needed to play it, as I did not have the money to begin renting somewhere. Game on!

And so it went. While enduring constant harassment from unsecured (read credit card) debtors, I waited and watched for signs from my mortgage company. Finally in late September, the letter came. They were serious and they had hired an attorney to proceed with the foreclosure process. The required four weeks of legal notice in the local newspaper would commence in October, with a sale date set for the first Tuesday in November. First shot fired.

I began in earnest searching out ways to pay my attorney to file my bankruptcy prior to the end of October to fend of the impending sale of my house. This was no small feat…as it was more money than I had seen in one place for many many months! The first Wednesday in October, there it was—my house listed in the legal section of the local paper. There was no escaping what was happening now…I had been outed by the legal notice. There was no more hiding—everyone in my neighborhood knew what was happening. While I had confided in a few close friends, the vast majority of the people I knew, including most of my family, had no clue how bad things really were. Now it was right out there for everyone to read in the paper.

As the month of October sped along, I began to get desperate. I knew that I had to come up with $3,000 to pay the attorney before he would file on my behalf. The only thing of solid value that I still owned was my beloved little convertible (see front cover). I had purchased this car from an employee back in 1996 and loved every minute of owning it. It was a second car, but it embodied and expressed my free spirit and my life philosophy, especially the bumper stickers. I really enjoyed this car.

Well, you guessed it....that car became my get out of jail free card. Or, more appropriately, it became the ticket that bought my way into legal bankruptcy. Some very dear friends had expressed an interest in my beloved little convertible several months back, but that was back when I was still convinced that I was going to figure this whole thing out. When the magic didn't happen and the clock was about to expire, I called them and asked if they still had an interest. They came later that same day and bought my Miata for $3,500. Thanks Adlen & Paul.

I made the appointment that very same day to do the paperwork to file.

I filed for bankruptcy on Halloween in 2008. It was really a very simple process. I listed all of my creditors and all of my assets. As I had previously feared, this is not a process where you list every piece of clothing you own and give the court permission to take possession of it. The list only included a very broad brush of things that I owned. The court is only looking at things that could be considered as part of an asset sale. They DO NOT want your grandmother's silverware. They are, however, interested in a boat that you may have parked somewhere or a house in the Caymans. Anything that you own that could be sold for a substantial gain is part of the equation....the little stuff isn't even considered. Again, they do not want your fur coat.

I drove away from the attorney's office in my one remaining car with a sense of depression, failure...and then exuberance! It was all going to stop! All the harassing phone calls would end as soon as the letters were received by my creditors. Legally, the minute you file in the courts, a "silent period" beings. From this point forward, none of your creditors is allowed to contact you directly. All communications must go through your attorney. The water boarding torture of constant, relentless phone calls, letters and urgent deliveries was going to stop! And, most importantly, so did the clock that was ticking towards the November foreclosure sale on my house!

My attorney's best advice was that I would most likely be able to stay in my house until the first Tuesday in February....maybe March, depending on how quickly the courts would move in my case. With the clock reset, I was now kicked out of the inertia induced coma I needed to develop a plan to find a place to live…and a way to pay for it by sometime early in the new year. At least I had a schedule now.

My previously stuffed mailbox now was filled only with utility bills and magazines. Even my regular car payment statements for 2007 Chevy I was driving stopped coming. I was told by my attorney's office that this was the way it was supposed to be…and that statements would restart when the decision of the court was passed down. I was free….at least for a few months. Silence really is golden…

One side note here—when you are filing for bankruptcy, make sure that you list anyone and everyone who is or might be a potential creditor! I meticulously went back through my records to list anyone who might claim to have an action against me…including a shopping center where I had previously operated a business. This particular landlord had required me to sign a personal guarantee of the lease. While I was no longer operating this business, the person whom I had sold it to was, by all reports, not doing well. On the outside chance that this personal guarantee could be revisited, I listed this landlord on my list of creditors given to my attorney. As luck would have it, before the letters were actually mailed, I received an action from this landlord, naming me in a lawsuit against the current owner of the business for back rent. Whew….dodged a bullet on that one! Letters went out—and that was the end of that!

So a word of caution…if you are going this route, take the time to dust off the cobwebs and think through the process! If there is anyone/organization out there that you think might have a claim against you, GET THEM ON THE LIST!

And another thing—DO NOT sign anything during the period between your filing for bankruptcy and the date that your bankruptcy is discharged! By doing so, it may or may not be included in the bankruptcy proceeding. Best case, any legal document you sign during this period is considered null & void by the courts. Worst case, you could be held accountable and something that you thought was included in your filing may be pulled into present day!

Case in point, an unsecured loan that I held through a local bank had been in default and the bank officer was looking to get it off the monthly delinquent loan listing at his bank. (This was NOT the loan held by the wonderful friend of mine who demonstrated such understanding when I went to him with the truth early in 2008!). However, this officer was taking heat from the board of directors and had asked that I help him out by restructuring so he could take this off the default list. He wanted me to extend the payback schedule, with payment being made as a lump sum at some point in the future. Seemed legit—he would be off the hook and life would go on. This friendly request was reiterated by the bank president on more than one occasion, just help them out and get this off their heat list. But upon further investigation, I was told that if I had indeed signed this type of agreement, this loan might well have been pulled out of my bankruptcy…and I would be looking for ways to repay it! Whew….

So what happens next, you may wonder. Well, the first thing you have to do is complete a bankruptcy course. Most attorneys are able to offer this to you online (they probably even make some money on it?), but it is quicker and faster that way. You simply log in to designated site with the information your attorney provides and begin! It's much like taking an online survey—there are no trick questions or lengthy forms to fill out. Just click and roll. You'll need to go all the way through to get the confirmation # they provide, although they must send the information directly to your attorney as well. Nothing scary about that part.

During the filing of my Chapter 7 bankruptcy, I was only required to appear in court one time. I had been to one of these court appearances once a few years earlier, where I was chasing down a builder who had taken my money and left me high and dry. It was very intimidating. The appearance was in a very large courtroom in front of an imposing judge who ruled over the proceedings from an elevated position. In this case, the judge's voice boomed out that this individual was filing for bankruptcy and that anyone in the courtroom who had an interest in this case should make themselves known. It was just like in the movies. I was really dreading this appearance.

My notice came in mid-November, listing December 29th as the appearance date. Happy Holidays! My attorney assured me that we could delay the proceedings, as I was headed to Chicago for Christmas. But in the end, I decided that there might be an advantage to this date....it was the week between Christmas and New Year's, after all! How many people would be around to witness this disgrace? I decided to keep the date and get it over with.

On the way home from Chicago two days after Christmas, I received an e-mail from my attorney with a forward from the bankruptcy trustee's office. Due to the "complications" in my case, this office was requesting additional records. As though completely unrelated to the court appearance date, further documentation was being requested. I was given 10 days to furnish the court with copies of every statement from every creditor (both secured and unsecured) from every month for the past 16 months! I was freaking out! Of course, this type of e-mail never comes during the business day...or even during the business week!

And when do you think this e-mail arrived? On Saturday night in a hotel room where we had stopped during the drive from Chicago to Atlanta in order to make it home for the court appearance! Nothing I could do until Monday morning. More ulcers in the making!

In the end, I did get a two-week extension on this request from the court, but the appearance on the 29th went ahead as scheduled. I drove to the courthouse that day with full dread on.

Imagine my surprise when I entered the room and was directed to a small room at the end of a narrow hallway. No intimidating courtroom scene. No judge sitting aloft with an intimidating microphone. Just a room filled to overflowing capacity with over 60 other souls suffering the same fate as mine. A small table sat in the middle of the room, where the bankruptcy trustee sat interviewing candidates for bankruptcy. I was floored. Her voice was barely audible in the old room with low ceilings and tattered carpet as she probed the facts in each case. "Is this the first time you have filed for bankruptcy" "Are you currently employed" "Do you have any assets not listed here" "Do you swear to tell the whole truth and nothing but the truth, so help you God?"

When it was my turn, my attorney and I proceeded to the head of the room. She asked a few questions about my current business venture. Was I taking the fall for a business partner (if only!). Were there any assets that had not been listed here? Was my house on the market? Did I wish to reaffirm the loan on my home (ha!) Did I have any type of paying job in addition to my current business venture? All in all, pretty run of the mill stuff. I answered the questions, she was kind, it was over.

Leaving the courtroom, my attorney told me that he had received correspondence from the lien holder on my 2007 Chevy. It was the reaffirmation agreement. This paperwork was what was needed in order to reaffirm the loan and keep the car. Up until now, I had thought this was simply a process of agreeing to continue to make payments. It was not.

In order to reaffirm, my attorney had to testify that I had the means to continue to make the payments. At this point, I had been looking in earnest for a paying job since late October, but had been completely unable to find ANYTHING! He informed me that unless I could prove that I had income (through pay stubs)…he would be unable to attest to my ability to repay this loan! Further, he stated, that if he were unable to testify to the reaffirmation, the judge certainly would not, and this would leave the loan within the realm of the bankruptcy! OMG! For the first time, I now was faced with the reality that I might lose my car too! And this just two short months after selling my beloved little convertible to finance the bankruptcy! I had to have a car! What was I going to do!

We left the courthouse with this issue unresolved. My attorney told me that I had until late February to be able to prove to him that I had the means to continue to pay the car payments going forward and thereby reaffirm the loan. Good thing I was an expert at living with stress at this point!

Just so you know, the same thing is true with reaffirming your house in a bankruptcy. It isn't simply a matter of you saying, "Why, yes! I would like to reaffirm this mortgage and keep my house!" You must prove to the court (and, by the way, to your attorney if they are scrupulous!), that you have enough regular income to make ongoing payments. Enough, at least in my case, was considered to be not more than 31% of my regular income. Since my regular income was zero, this was an easy calculation for me! But you might want to keep this in mind if you should decided that you do want to keep your house!

So…you think you might want to keep your house? You couldn't have picked a better time! With the current state of the economy and the number of foreclosures rising every month, banks and mortgage holders have never been more willing to talk. Actually, some are so behind, they don't even have time to talk! Remember, I tried to call my mortgage company months before filing for bankruptcy…and they continually told me to wait until I was behind. When I was behind several months, for that matter!), they still wouldn't talk to me. In the end, it was over a year and a half from last mortgage payment to actual foreclosure. That gives you LOTS of time to talk!

Here's the key…YOU must be the driver in this ongoing conversation. DO NOT rely on your bank/mortgage company to seek you out. But here's the good news—if you are proactive, the bank will most likely be more than willing to work with you.

Current statistics say that it costs the average mortgage holder more than $75,000 to move through the foreclosure process on an individual home. If they can work with you to avoid that, they will likely be miles ahead. Pick up the phone, write letters, follow-up…do whatever you need to do to get their attention and make this work! Don't just ignore the elephant in the room—you'll wake up one day and see that the elephant has knocked down the walls!

If you decide that keeping your house is not an option (or not in your best interest)….here are some things to think about. The most important message here is again—communicate!! With a hard asset like a home that can be taken from you if you don't pay the note, it is critical that you talk as much and as often as possible to reach the best possible outcome for both parties. That being said, if you don't want (or can't afford) to keep your house, call your mortgage company!!   There are solutions somewhat less severe than foreclosure.

Consider a deed in lieu of foreclosure. This is a legal instrument where you convey all interest in your home to your lender to satisfy a loan that is in default and thereby avoid the whole process of foreclosure. This process offers several advantages to both you and the lender. The principal advantage to you is that it immediately releases you from most or all of the personal indebtedness associated with the loan that is in default. And even though bankruptcy is becoming more commonplace, this process will avoid the public notoriety of a foreclosure proceeding and you may receive more generous terms than you would in a formal foreclosure. Another benefit to you is that it hurts your credit less than a foreclosure does. The obvious advantages to your lender include a reduction in the time and cost of the repossession. Not a bad solution!

One big word of caution on this type of transaction!!! If you aren't careful, they could slip in one little piece of paper into the pile that you are signing that says that they are going to bill you for the difference between what they can reasonably expect to get for your home on the open market and the amount of your mortgage. So, let's just say that you owe about....say....$400,000 for your house (hmmm...wonder who that was??), and your house is currently worth about $268,000. A deed in foreclosure or a short sale COULD result in you owing the difference!!!

Giver back, beware!!!

There is something else called "jingle mail" that is happening a lot these days. This is when the homeowner simply mails the keys back to the mortgage company. Seems easy enough, but sort of a cop out. Much better to talk it out. There are some solutions that might even allow you to stay in your house if you have a job and both parties are willing to work it out!

If the foreclosure train is coming, you should still continue to talk! It was suggested to me that I even talk with the mortgage company about becoming a tenant in my own home. While it may sound bizarre, the idea makes sense! If the mortgage company knows that they are going to foreclose, why not offer to stay, pay a reasonable rent amount and maintain the home while they move through the legal process and on to selling the house. You would certainly have to remain flexible about the term of your tenancy, but it could offer you a way to stay in your house longer with the blessing of your mortgage company!

CHAPTER 9

"Just Like Starting Over"

Crawling Out

As the months marched on, I knew it was simply a matter of time before I lost the house. Rather than wait for the mortgage company to have first mover advantage, I decided that I needed to get moving (literally!) and find a place to live. My biggest fear was that we would end up in a double wide…or the car! Who was going to rent to someone who had no money, no job and an impending bankruptcy?

But, as I've said before, I'm an eternal optimist…and I knew I would eventually begin the crawl out. I was feverishly searching for a job…any kind of job…but was severely limited due to the fact that my son was in a school that was out of our district for the past two years. This meant that I had to drive him back and forth to school every day. I knew that had to change so I could be free to take whatever job came along. And I knew I had to get out of that house. The whole scene was just too depressing.

I began a search in earnest for a rental located in my son's school district. At first, I started calling around on rentals from the local paper. Once they requested information on my employment situation, things usually went downhill pretty quickly. My credit score was decimated, so that didn't help either. My search started in December of 2008, and by February of 2009, things were starting to look pretty bleak.

It finally occurred to me that I needed an advocate. My first phone call was to a friend of mine who is a realtor (and currently had my house listed…in hopes of a short-sale offer). She started pulling up rentals in the local MLS listing and began in earnest to research the particulars. Perhaps we could find someone who was in foreclosure and could use rental income to save their house. Maybe we could luck on an out-of-state owner who just needed someone in the house short term until they could sell. Clearly, we were in need of an unusual situation.

After a few weeks of feverishly searching, she decided that we should take a look at a new subdivision that had just been built behind my son's (soon-to-be) high school. As I mentioned earlier, he had been attending a middle school that was out of district for two years, and this was the high school that his middle school would funnel into. Brand new? A house? Are you kidding me??

We went and looked anyway—what did I have to lose, right?? It was beautiful....a small, one street subdivision very similar to the one I was being foreclosed out of, with about 14 houses that LITERALLY backed up to the high school! I couldn't believe that we might actually have a shot!

My realtor proceeded to deal with the onsite broker. Since she is in the biz, I let her handle the details of the offer. We low-balled an offer to lease (the houses were for sale only at this point), and asked for everything. She included everything from stainless steel appliances to lawn maintenance, plus her commission! Seemed unlikely to me, but, hey, she was the expert!

Did I mention I learned yet another valuable lesson here? A few days went by and we heard nothing. Finally, I decided to call the onsite agent myself to follow-up. Turns out that he presented the offer to the developer who became so aggravated that he literally THREW the offer across the room! OMG! Talk about a backfire! The agent told me that the deal was all but dead. I was devastated.

With time not on my side and my desperation rising, I asked him what he thought I could do. His suggestion was the best I had heard to date...call the developer myself and ask for a meeting. So that is exactly what I did. I called, explained who I was, that the real estate broker was now out of the deal and pleaded with him to meet with me. After much convincing, he agreed.

This was one of the most humbling, hat-in-hand experiences I had to endure to date. I knew that I had absolutely NO bargaining power and that my chances of being successful were very slim. I decided to play the game like the pros....and go on the offense.

The first thing I did was make copies of my personal & business tax returns for several years when my income was well into the six figures. My thinking was that he needed to know that I was not just the total of my current credit score. I had to convince him that my current situation was short-lived and that I was resourceful enough to dig my way out.

The second thing I did was pull up all the comparable rentals within a 1 mile radius of the property. While our original offer was a low-ball, I knew that the price he was asking for rent was a good $200-$300 over current market value. I was in a bad situation, but I wasn't about to get snookered. And, by the way, I couldn't afford the higher rate (could I afford anything??).

My final step in preparing for this meeting was to do a little research on the developer himself. The Internet is an amazing thing...and I was able to see how many empty properties in numerous subdivisions they were sitting on throughout the Atlanta metro area. A banker friend of mine was able to tell me what kind of loans the company had outstanding, so I knew that they were pressed for immediate cash flow. I was ready.

On the day that we met, I entered the office prepared to eat major crow. My comps and my tax returns in hand, I thanked him profusely for meeting with me. I immediately apologized for the "ridiculous" offer that was made on my behalf by my realtor and assured him that she was no longer involved in the deal. I was desperate. A single mom with a bankruptcy in motion and no net under the tightrope I was walking, I really needed someone to give me a chance.

Then I pulled out my tax returns. I wanted him to know that, in spite of my current situation, I was capable of making a comfortable six-figure income...and these tax returns proved that. 13+ years of entrepreneurial endeavors proved that I wasn't simply at the mercy of a job offer. And look at the bright side—no job meant I couldn't get fired!! I promised him on my son that I was going to make something happen.

Then came the comps. Without any arrogance, I pulled these out, simply as a means to let him know that he was higher than his local competition. I went beyond that to explain that I was only able to afford a monthly rental amount in the range of the comps I had brought with me...but I really had a strong desire to be in his subdivision.

Finally, I used the last thing I had in my currently limited bag of tricks. Most of my career success has come from some level of marketing expertise in almost every endeavor. Whether selling ideas, things or people, I have a strong track record of knowing how to put things in the best light to move things along. So I offered him something he needed. In exchange for his consideration, I offered to help him market his subdivisions. While I am not a licensed real estate agent (although I used to be!), I could still assist in marketing outreach, stirring up leads and showing properties. I could be the onsite person to handle things that would otherwise cost him money to take care of.

I couldn't tell you which of the above tactics worked the best—all I know is that by the time I left, he agreed to rent me the house I wanted at a price I thought I could afford. The same man who had thrown my previous offer across the table was now thanking me for coming in to meet with him. He went on to say that he normally has to make decisions based solely on the numbers on paper. But after meeting me and hearing my story, he decided that I was sorely in need of someone who would give me a break. And so he did.

The rest of the story is that he needed a down payment. When I told him that I had no cash, he asked if I had anything left of value that he could hold as collateral. By this time, the only thing that I hadn't sold was my diamond tennis bracelet (I couldn't sell that either!) . It was not for lack of trying, but I had been unable to sell this piece of jewelry through all the varied websites and people I had offered it through. This 5 carat bracelet had some sentimental value….it was the replacement that the insurance company had offered me for my mother's wedding ring that had been stolen 5 years earlier (see! This story did not just begin at the beginning of the bankruptcy!!). But times were desperate, like I had never envisioned…and I offered it up. He agreed to have it appraised and write up the lease.

In the end, he told me that he didn't need the tennis bracelet. I now wear it almost every day as a reminder of where I was and how far I've come….

What you drive says a lot about you, right? (ha!)

So we started plans to move in to our brand new 5-bedroom home on April 1st. Yes, that's right…a BRAND NEW 5-bedroom home—a home that literally backs up to my son's high school. For the first time ever, he could walk to school! Now I was free to search for any kind of employment during any hours…I wasn't tied to driving him back and forth to school, football practice, etc. It was exhilarating! We were crawling out!!

But wait, there's more! About that same time, while I was recovering from freaking out about finding a place to live, I got a call from GMAC, the holders of my then current car loan on the 2007 Chevrolet HHR I was driving. Remember that I had sold my convertible to pay the attorney to file my bankruptcy the previous October, so this was my only car...and I had to have a car!

The call from GMAC was to tell me that I was nearly $2,000 in arrears on my car loan. When I told them my understanding of not paying car payments while in the midst of bankruptcy, the quickly told me that I was incorrect. Just because they weren't sending me payment coupons didn't mean that I wasn't supposed to making payments! Yickes!

You see my understanding was that once the bankruptcy was granted, the car payments would pick up where we left off prior to filing and the life of the loan would be extended to include the original 60 months. Boy was I wrong. I was now behind more than five months, and if I didn't come up with the cash, they were coming for the car.

Remember that I had not been able to officially "reaffirm" the car loan in my bankruptcy proceedings. Without regular income, which I still didn't have, the court wouldn't endorse that action. Now I was in trouble.

I asked them what options I had. With a little research, they determined that the clock had run out for me to reaffirm. The bankruptcy was now so close to being discharged that no further actions could be run through the court system. GMAC's best answer was that I could pay the arrears and continue to make my monthly payments, even though I would not legally own the car. At the end of the loan term, they would still mail me the title, but until then, I would not be the legal owner of record. Are you kidding me??? Thinking this might be my only option, I asked them to put that in writing. They refused.

Panic struck again. I told them that I needed to consult my attorney so I could get off the phone. What I really needed to do was run to the bathroom and throw up. I had to have a car!

After a few minutes, I regained my composure and went to work. My first call was to the main office of the U.S. Bankruptcy Court Northern District of Georgia. (Even though my case was filed in a different court in a different city, all final discharges come from this office, I now know! I searched through all my paperwork and e-mails to discover that little fact!). They told me that my case had cleared all the hurdles and that the discharge would be issued any day. It was true—time was up.

Typical for me, I began gathering facts. I wasn't sure where I was going to get the money for the arrears, but first I needed to be sure that keeping the car was the right decision. My first move was to go to CarMax and get an appraisal. That number came back at about $7,500—significantly less than the $13,000 I still owed on the car. I searched Kelly Blue Book (www.KBB.com) and Edmunds (www.Edmunds.com) to verify the number. Not too far off. The mileage on the car was just over 50,000 miles, meaning it was out of warranty. Trying to work to keep the car seemed more and more like a bad idea.

Then, as if on queue, the power steering went out. Now I was driving a car that drove like a truck that was out of warranty. I called the dealership and was told that this could be a fuse…or it could be an expensive power steering motor. Gone are the days of adding power steering fluid. It was something electronic.

So began my search for another car. Let me tell you that trying to get approved for a car loan at this point in my life was the closest thing to impossible that I could imagine. I quickly learned that no dealership would approve me until I had the proof of the discharge in my hand. Smart business people do not want to take the chance that their new loan will end up in the pile of discharged debts when the final gavel hits. That just made the impossible search even more impossible. Now I was racing the clock.

As I searched for a car...or more appropriately for a dealership that would consider loaning me the money, I continued to call the Bankruptcy Court every day to see if the final discharge papers were in hand.

I spoke to dealerships all over the country...literally! I figured I would be money ahead to try and scrape up the money to fly somewhere and drive a car home than pay off the arrears and keep the car that wouldn't legally belong to me anymore. I scanned E-Bay, put an appeal for a loan on Craig's List, called my banker friend...you name it, I did it.

Back before I got the call from GMAC, I had looked around a bit for a car. I knew that I was upside down on this car (although not as much as I later learned that I was!), so I occasionally did an online search for wagons. Laugh if you will, but I was pretty convinced that I needed to keep driving something with a storage area...just in case it became home for a while. So initially I limited my search for used wagons within a 50-mile radius of where I lived.

Wouldn't you know that the first car that came up was a 2005 Jaguar station wagon? Who knew that Jaguar made a station wagon? The car was beautiful and met my criteria for storage and uniqueness. And it was at a sports car dealership about 40 miles from my house! I was in love.

Of course I went to look at it. I didn't drive it, just drove by and looked at it. After I got home, I called and spoke to the sales guy who told me that he would work with me, but I would have to have the discharge of bankruptcy notification in hand before we could proceed. I didn't go any further.

Finding this unique car did lead me to many other searches. Turns out wagons were a pretty limited edition thing with Jaguar, and I had owned a 1985 Jaguar back that I loved and owned for 13 years. So wherever I found one, I called. I talked to dealerships from Atlanta to Ohio to California. They were all either flawed (previous accidents, etc) and/or more money than the one near my house.

Still, I went through the motions of loan approval, supposing that my bankruptcy was already discharged. Here's where the door slammed in my face. No one would loan me money…and who could blame them! I broadened my search to include any kind of wagon. Still, no one was willing to make the loan.

I had some pretty soul-searching conversations with myself. What was I going to do? How could I get a loan? Where would the money come from to bring the loan on the HHR current so they wouldn't repossess it? The 2005 Jaguar never was far from the back of my mind. My dear friend Donna forced me to look at things objectively. I couldn't drive to pick up food stamps in a Jaguar, could I? I hate that objective logic that she always brings to the table!!!

The day that I received word that my case had been discharged, I made plans to go downtown and pick up my files. The very nice woman whom I had been checking with for several days told me that she was going to place a copy of the discharge letter in the stack of files, even though she wasn't supposed to. Not having to wait for this proof to come in the mail gave me a couple of precious extra days to see if I could pull this out. I called the sports car dealership back.

Yes, the Jaguar was still there. No, there was no coming off the price. We had gotten to the bottom number already and I hadn't even driven the car yet! But I was not about to waste time running around when I was so close to not having a car to drive! I informed him that I had the discharge letter and asked him if he would please put the application in with their lender to see if there was any hope. He did. There was.

After a call to me to confirm the facts and understand my situation, the lending officer called the dealership and approved the loan. Don't ask me how or why…all I know is that the only place in the U.S. that I was able to find that would approve a car loan for me was the one that this dealership used.

You should know that I was going to pay a price for this loan. The interest rate that they offered was a full 18%. I know that seems ridiculous, particularly since the loan on the HHR was at 0%. But here are the facts. I was now upside down nearly $7,000 on the HHR. The Jaguar was valued by Kelley Blue Book and Edmunds at nearly $18,000 and we had agreed on a purchase price of only $14,000. So, same loan amount, but for a car that would exceed the value of the loan. Seemed to make sense to me.

There still was that little issue of coming up with enough money down to keep my car payments the same. I knew I would have to have a car payment, and the entire transaction seemed logical if I could keep my payments the same. I agreed to go over and drive the car that Friday afternoon when my son was out of school.

Of course we both feel in love! This was the kind of car that I had driven most of his life…and mine—a solid, well-built, beautiful car. When we sat down to discuss the numbers, the down payment that I thought I could scrounge up was $500 less equity than the lender had stated was needed. We went through every possible scenario, but there seemed to be no answer. So I went for broke; I pleaded with the sales guy to call the bank back. He resisted, saying that they had been very firm about the amount of down payment needed. Plus he didn't think this person would be around at 5p.m. on a Friday afternoon. But I begged him to call them anyway.

Like so many things that have happened to me in my life, I will never understand how this happened. The call went to the cell phone of the lending officer, who just happened to be sitting in her boss's office at that moment. Since he would be the one who

would have to approve this exception, she put him on speakerphone. With the wave of his hand, he approved the exception and the loan was approved right on the spot.

I told the sales guy that it wouldn't be until Wednesday that I would be able to come up with the required amount. He told me to write a post-dated check and take the car home.

As unbelievable as this may sound, on that very day, the repo-man was in my driveway. My neighbor saw him out there and he came over and asked if she had seen me or the HHR. She freaked out and started calling to see if she could find me and tell me not to come home! What a good friend. Thanks Nancy.

I left the HHR on the lot of that sports car dealership and told them that a tow truck would be coming to retrieve it. The next morning, I called the repo company and gave them the address. It was that close.

So it came to be that at exactly the same time we were planning on moving into our brand new house, we became the owners of a 2005 Jaguar. My car payments remained at just under $300 a month. Life was good.

I Owe, I Owe, So off to Work I Go:

Okay, so now I really needed a job. My dear friend and business partner was now working for a consultant business in the dental industry and thought she could finagle something for me where I couldn't do much damage, as I had NO history in dental. She was able to convince the woman that owned the company that I was smart, had been successful and would figure it out. By the next week, I found myself working in a dental office for $17 an hour.

Remember that this would not have been possible any earlier than it happened! I was now only days away from moving into the school district that would allow my son to walk or take the bus to school. My friend made the appropriate excuses to allow me to come in late and leave early until we got moved. I started full time April 1st. (April Fool's Day…there's that irony again!)

I did my best to keep a gratitude journal during most of this experience. There really was so much to be grateful for. I can't tell you how many times a bill came due that I didn't have the money for, and suddenly, a check would arrive from nowhere. A rebate from several months earlier. A deposit returned from a utility company where a former business was located that I didn't know I had coming. Needing to purchase tires and coming home to realize that something I had listed on Craig's List had sold for almost that exact amount. Or the check that arrived in the mail from my wonderful niece just in time to make a car payment that I couldn't afford to make that month (Thanks Jenny & Cliff). The series of events that occurred was simply nothing short of miraculous.

The timing continued to work like this through the time that I worked at this job. I had to wait 90 days for health insurance to kick in. In mid-June I received a letter that I had reached the earnings threshold for Medicaid coverage and that my benefits would expire on June 30th. My employer paid health insurance kicked in July 1st.

To look at us from the outside, I'm sure everyone thought that we were on top of the world! Here we were, living in a brand new house driving a Jaguar! The truth is that we were on top of the world...but it wasn't because of the material things we had. We had made it through and seemed to be crawling out of the end of the tunnel. And we were still okay. More than okay. And I had yet another "teachable experience" to talk with my son about. Don't judge. Things are not always what they seem to be from the outside.

CHAPTER 10

"Here Comes the Sun"

THE BEGINNING...

So, you may ask, did I finally get the lesson? All these years of struggle...and suddenly it became so clear. The lesson I needed to learn all along is not simply knowing when to turn things over to God—it is that I wasn't ever in control to begin with! It is not about deciding when...it's about letting God be in charge continuously. All those years I've struggled to make things work, to make the right decisions, to keep things moving forward—I've had it upside down. I am not in charge. A tough lesson for a classic Type A!

Remember those little finger traps we had as kids? You'd stick your index fingers into the ends of it and then try to pull them out. The more you struggled, the more impossible it became to release your fingers from the trap. If you didn't know the secret of these little things, you'd struggle and panic, pulling harder and harder to get your fingers out.

The "secret" with these turns out to be very simple. Don't struggle. Just like the teachings of Taoism, Christianity and countless other religions, both "new age" and old school…simply follow the flow of the universe. Let go and let God. The more you struggle against the tide, the harder your life will become. Live harmoniously with your surroundings and your life will seem effortless and your soul will be in seamless synch with the rest of the world.

As I write, I am sitting on the courthouse steps watching the foreclosure sale of my home of thirteen years. There is an air of excitement, as potential bidders troll from person to person, trying to determine if they represent the law firm that is auctioning off the property they are there to bid on.

Questions are flying about specific property addresses…is the house they came for still on the "active" list? You see, just because it is advertised in the "legals" section of the paper doesn't mean that it made it to the steps on the date of the sale. Last minute deals, short sale offers, bankruptcy filings….all sorts of things can bring a halt to a specific property auction.

2009/11/03 10:04

So, if you are interested, here's how the process works. There is no big pronouncement with an auctioneer standing at the top of the courthouse steps, megaphone in hand. Instead, each attorney's office that has advertised properties in the "legals" sends a representative who simply walks into the crowd with a clipboard. They pronounce which law firm they represent and start reading off property addresses, identifications, tract #s, etc. Then it begins.

It is all stunningly quiet. Everyone huddles around the person with the clipboard, leaning in to hear which law firm they represent, which property they are on, what is the opening bid. It's hard to hear for all the street noise. There are many seasoned pros here, clearly. Then there is the occasional newbie, wandering around trying to figure out what is going on.

Anyone with a clipboard appears to be an authority. The short man in the baseball cap continues to drone on until the list of properties is exhausted. Then the crowd shifts to circle the next one. Cashier's checks in excess of $100,000 are handed over like trading cards, all the while the wind is blowing (now we know why they have clipboards, I guess!). A handicapped man in Army fatigues, an unkempt gray beard and a baseball cap forks over $70,000 in Cashier's checks, 1/3 of the price he just bid to acquire a property. The auctioneer clearly knows this man—they've done this before. It's all too depressing…I had to leave.

In the end, it took my mortgage company one year and 5 months to finally foreclose. I guess I was the beneficiary of the times, extensions granted because of the economic times, but I never expected that it would take that long. In some ways, I wish it would have happened more quickly…I was ready to move on and wanted that chapter in my life to be over. But as I sat there on November 3, 2009, watching a very unceremonious end to this nightmare, I didn't really feel anything. No shame, no remorse, no emotion at all.

By the way, if you are in the same situation as I was with little or no communication from the lender and unsure about where things stand, I would recommend signing up for alerts on your property with Eproperty Watch. This is a service that will notify you if there is a change of legal ownership of your home. Signing up is easy and free...and even if you are not in the throws of foreclosure, but just want to be sure that your title is secure, it's a great resource to have. (www.EpropertyWatch.com).

I remember as a child being afraid of the dark. I have vivid memories of walking down the short hallway in our small house to my bedroom, consumed with fear. I can even remember times as an adult, afraid to go downstairs in my own house in the middle of the night, fearing the unknown. Funny, because now I have absolutely no fear of the dark. I can't even recall the feeling. I can't tell you exactly when this changed...it has just become evident over time. I'm just not afraid anymore...

Adversity has a strange way forcing you to re-connect—with yourself, with your loved ones and with the world. During the three years that my son was "out of district" and had to be driven to school everyday, our morning commute took us past a group of middle school kids waiting each morning for the bus. On sunny days, they stood scattered, chatting, kicking the dirt—some alone, some chatting with one or two others. But on the days there was rain, a whole different group dynamic occurred. All of the kids huddled tightly together, using the strength of the group against the weather.   If there was one person with an umbrella, he or she was at the center…and the group huddled even more tightly.   That, my friend, is why adversity exists in the world.

I now wonder if my old life was the blessing or the curse. Jetting around from place to place in private planes, running hard and fast, and getting used to the exceptions that the world makes for busy people…I got sucked in.   But now I know that it was then that I was only existing.   Today I have a rich & full life, full of blessings, friends, loved ones and meaning.   There is always a reason to feel like less if you are comparing yourself to someone else.   The only definition of YOU should be from within…between you and your maker.   Nothing else really matters.

Like most Americans, I can remember exactly where I was on 9/11.   I was working from home, getting ready to fly to New York for a speaking engagement.   I had the television on (as always!), but the sound was off, as I was finalizing a presentation I had to give on my way to the airport.   Earlier in the day than usual, my niece called.   When I picked up the phone, she said, "You aren't still planning on going to New York, are you?"   Of course, I said…I had places to go and people to see!   She suggested that I turn the sound on.

As I sat there, staring in horror at the acts of that day, the only thing in the world that seemed important to me was my then

6-year old son. He was at school less than a mile away…and perfectly safe. But that didn't matter. I got in the car and drove to school to have lunch with him. Entering the cafeteria, I could see that I wasn't the only mom struck with this instinct. Several of us exchanged knowing glances as we sat with our little ones who

were blissfully unaware of what was taking place that day. As the world experienced a cosmic shift, sitting there with my son was the only thing that mattered. I'm certain that this scene played out all across America that day.

So even though he doesn't have a college fund, I know my son will be fine. His soul is good…and I've done my best to instill the right things into his consciousness while he is in my charge. I do know that the past few years have changed him, but I don't think the changes have been bad. As a matter of fact, I think he will now grow up to be a strong man who knows adversity and, more importantly, knows you can come out on the other side—damaged, repaired and stronger in the broken places. Together, we will find a way for him to set the course for him to achieve whatever he sets out to do in life.

I know that a lot of people have gone through some serious readjustments over the past year or two. People (like me!) who never dreamed that they would be one of the "working poor" have found themselves unable to make house payments, losing jobs that they had held for years...struggling in ways that they could never have previously imagined. The near fatal case of AFFLUENZA that we all had at the turn of the century has been miraculously cured! And though the cure was painful, the end result will be good for all of us.

The job that I got just in time for us to make the bold move into our new house is now gone. Under-employment leads to some strange circumstances. A small company with a smart but insecure & unsaavy owner led to a no-win situation for me. The harder I worked to make the practice succeed, the more she was convinced that I was up to something. She knew of my 'successful' history and made sure that I knew that I was not going to be successful in her organization. I started out checking insurance in the corner for $17 an hour...and seven months later was the 'go-to' person for everyone...still making $17 an hour. And suddenly, it came to an unceremonious end. She simply called me in, sat me down and it was over. Of course, she didn't have the courage to tell me that directly. I finally had to say, "So...I know you don't want me here. How can we resolve this?" Within 10 minutes, I was walking out the door with all my personal possessions and two weeks severance pay. That meant that I was two weeks away from not having enough money to survive. No thanks Gina.

So, yes, I'm back on food stamps while I try to figure out what to do next. It is of little solace to me that she hired two people to replace me, and the practice is struggling. I do qualify for unemployment this time, so at least I have a little cushion that didn't exist a year ago. I do know that my son and I will survive. I've never doubted that for even a moment. While my risk tolerance is higher than most, I have always known deep down that whatever came my way, I would find my way out. No matter what...**I'm still here.**

The higher purpose of sharing my experience is to present a micro chasm of the meaning of life. No matter how bad things are...good is there, if you look hard enough. And the good times...well, that's no guarantee that bad stuff doesn't still happen.

When I couldn't bear to go back to my old house, my friends worked together to pull a garage sale together with items that still remained. The sale netted me over $500...and some trouble. Apparently, one of the "shoppers" went through a few bags of garbage and found some old checks from long ago closed accounts. I know this because that very night I received a phone call from a sheriff's deputy in a neighboring county. He had found several books of these checks scattered along the highway. Police reports were filed and frantic calls to the banks involved were made first thing Monday morning. I was assured that there was no action I needed to take, as the accounts were closed.

You probably already guessed the rest. Within a few weeks, I was receiving notices from debt collectors trying to retrieve small amounts for pizza, groceries, etc. Yep, they were able to use these checks in small establishments around the county. Now I have been advised to check once a month with the Magistrate's office to be sure that there are no outstanding warrants for my arrest. I'm relieved to say that three months into it, I have not had the sheriff show up at my door with handcuffs…but believe me when I tell you that I will continue to check in monthly!

See…the good and the bad, all mixed up together in one big messy pile. That's life.

In 2008, more than one million Americans filed for personal bankruptcy. That is more than a 30% increase over 2007. It ain't over yet.

How can you bounce back from bankruptcy? It's not immediate, but it can happen. The forced purchase of my car in March of 2009 turned out to be one of the smartest moves I could make. Unlike continuing to pay on loans that were already established before your bankruptcy, a new loan is a giant step towards reestablishing your credit. It is seen as your first step out…so make all your payments on time! A single late payment can set you back six months to a year in terms of your credit rating. Conversely, paying off more than the minimum payment can really help accelerate things.

It is likely that you will not be able to get a new credit card right away, but consider a "secured" credit card. This is a type of card where your credit line is equal to the amount that you pay to the bank/institution that issues the card (plus whatever fees they charge!). Make sure that the card issuer reports your new payment history to all three credit reporting agencies, as this will continue to help build your credit score. Some offers may include

hefty application fees and ridiculous interest rates, so be sure to check sites like Bankrate.com (www.BankRate.com) to search for the card with the best terms.

I am proud to tell you that my current credit score is 634!

(I know because I just checked it on Quizzle!!!). That's right...I'm ahead of my pre-bankruptcy, debt-laden score of 625!!! And this just over 7 months from the date that my bankruptcy was discharged! Why, you may ask! I now have no debt, except the loan on my car. That loan is paid EVERY month on time. So it makes me look like much more attractive in the eyes of the credit granting world. Very low debt, on time payments...and I can't file for bankruptcy again for 7+ years!

If you are still struggling with how you can come out on the other end, I would like to suggest an exercise that I put myself through after reading an article by Martha Beck in "O" magazine. It rang so true to me that I ripped out the page and have kept it with me ever since. On days where there seems to be more bad than good, I still pull it out.

Here's what Martha suggested to do when thoughts of scarcity persist:

1) List ten times you thought that there wouldn't be enough of something and you survived.

2) List ten areas where you have too much, not too little.

3) List 20—or 50, or 1,000—wonderful things that entered your life just at the right time, with no effort on your part.

I have a gratitude book that has a list of the reasons why I believe that miracles do happen. This was an exercise in the above. Just when things seemed completely hopeless, a check showed up from nowhere…a friend called…my niece gave me a word of encouragement, my son gave me a hug. It is all survivable…if you allow it.

Even in light of my current lack of employment, my son and I are traveling this Thanksgiving. You see, back when I was still working, I found a tremendous deal (LOVE to find those travel deals!!!) for a three day cruise for $99 a person. Yes, that's right, I said $99 a person! Being a complete optimist, I purchased this cruise deal in September, thinking that certainly things would be better by then. (Again with the unbridled optimism!!!). Little did I know that I would be back to being unemployed!

Fortunately, after finding the cruise, I continuously searched for airfare and was able to find one-way fares from Atlanta to Ft. Lauderdale for only $29 each...and $9 each way on the way back!!! Again, while still working, I purchased the tickets too. So as broke as we are, we are packing up and traveling (my favorite pastime) to south Florida to embark on a cruise for Thanksgiving this year. I wouldn't have it any other way!

So I'm off to find a way to keep us afloat...again, or still. At least for me, the tightrope is a little closer to the pavement this time. I'm not trying to find a way to balance hundreds of thousands of dollars of debt while walking my path. Things are much simpler now, but that doesn't mean that it will be easy.

Unemployment across the country is at an all time high. Most recent numbers have it just over 10% nationally, while some states are closer to 15% and climbing. The more interesting, yet significantly less publicized series of data known as U6. U6 is defined as *"total unemployed, plus all marginally attached workers plus total employed part-time for economic reasons, as a percent of all civilian labor force plus all marginally attached workers."* This is also referred to as the "misery index" (appropriately so!). This number is now hovering nationally at over 17%. To put that in relatable terms, one in every five people in the U.S. are currently experiencing the negative effects of some kind of job hit. That's a lot.

So here's where I give my pitch for enterpreneurialism. The best thing you can say about working for yourself is that you can't get fired! And more importantly, you are required to rely soley on yourself and your efforts to survive. As I said in the beginning, there's always been something very attractive to me about that. And after working a soul sucking job for seven months to survive, I am even more convinced that my future should be in my own hands.

Look around and see the need. Do you have friend or neighbors too busy to put up their holiday decorations? Hire yourself out! Do you make a killer cheesecake? Take some samples into local boutiques or coffee shops and see if they will sell them for you for a slice (hehehe) of the profits.

And most importantly, stay alert and flexible. I've gotten myself into a clinical trial, which involves me traveling about 45 minutes once per week to get poked, answer questions and give blood. What a feeling to walk out of there with $100 cash in my pocket!! And here's where the flexibility comes in...I drove straight from giving blood to the W Hotel to meet with a prospective client. Suck it up and do what you have to do.

As Zig Ziglar once said, "It is not the situation, but whether we react (negative) or respond (positive) to the situation that's important." (emphasis added). As I sit here putting the finishing touches on my story (at least so far), I recevied an e-mail with this quote in it. See how things work out???

"You are in the driver's seat of the journey of your life."

Drive carefully. ☺

EPILOUGE

2012

....and now the

REST of the story....

CHAPTER 11

"He Went out Tiger Hunting"

The Tables Have Turned

And so the story continues. Here I sit on a Mediterranean cruise. Okay, I know what you are thinking. It is now over three full years after that fateful day that I filed for bankruptcy. I wish I could tell you that things were fabulous and that I've made a complete return to the glory days. It just ain't so.

It's been a tough few years. Seems like the whole economy managed to land in the dumpster right on top of my personal situation. I always have been a trend setter ☺

However, the message once again is this…

I AM STILL STANDING!!!!

Remember the new house that I managed to rent from the builder by helping him market the subdivision? We loved that house...it was new, close to my son's school, perfect in almost every way. So when my two year lease was coming to and end, I began attempts to contact the landlord. I was ready to renew for another two years...just long enough to get my son out of high school.

Seemed a bit odd to me that the landlord was non-responsive, then vague, from January through March. My lease was set to expire on April 30th, and on March 30th he delivered the news. I received a certified letter—a communication mode that is ALWAYS some sort of bad news! The bank that held the loans on the unsold/leased houses in the subdivision had had enough and they were taking the houses back. I had an order to vacate on or before my lease termination date of April 30th.

Really?? I thought I was in good shape here, at least until my son got out of high school...but NO! Here we go again! So off I went on yet another search for yet another place to live and remain within my son's school district. I couldn't believe I was losing yet another house...and this wasn't even because I couldn't afford the rent!!!

Let me tell you...in the affluent suburbs north of Atlanta within a particularly overcrowded school, there was NOTHING to rent. I started out on yet another journey with a deadline...still carrying my financial baggage with me. When I finally did find a house that I could rent (because there was nothing except houses within the district), I was back to explaining my tale of woe to yet another potential landlord, trying to get approved.

Can I just tell how completely exhausting living in this state can be? I have often said that I feel like I have PTSD, without "post" part. Living on the absolute edge of a very high cliff for an extended period of time becomes a way of life that is at times debilitating and beyond description.

Allow me not to go back to where we left off...at the foreclosure auction of my home of 12+ years. No one bid that day, so my house went back to the bank that would never return my calls. Remember, I was early in this process. This was before the days of convention center cattle calls where "workout" specialists tried their best to figure out a way to modify your loan so the bank wouldn't have to take it back. With such a glut of houses on their books, banks are more amenable than ever to make every reasonable attempt to let you stay in your house. They wouldn't even answer my request to rent my own house until the foreclosure took place.

New programs like HARP even work with you to get you refinanced if you are "upside down" in your mortgage (owe more to the bank than the current market value of the house). Even other government programs are now allowing the previously unheard of practice of reducing your actual loan amount, not just your interest rate! All of this happened way too late for me.

At any rate, I walked away from the foreclosure auction that day in 2009 feeling strangely free, knowing that this particular chapter in my life was over. Now that I was no longer the legal owner of the house, any lingering fears of liability were now over. I worried that someone might break in to the house while it was vacant (remember, I moved out eight months before the actual foreclosure took place). Then if the house were left open, and a neighbor child ventured in and got hurt, would I be legally responsible?? Fortunately, those are issues I never received an education on...the house went back to the bank's ownership with the clap of the gavel that gloomy day in November. The circle was complete.

In the end, the bank had the house until they finally found a buyer, nearly two years later. After making the necessary repairs, painting the entire interior, maintaining the lawn and landscaping for 24 months, they sold my house in 2011 for only $195,000. Hard to believe that a house appraised for $430,000 in 2007 was sold for significantly less than I had paid for it originally in 1997. And my mortgage...remember that mortgage amount of $400,000??? Add attorney's fees and the cost of maintaining the house for two years while they looked for a buyer to that $200,000 loss, they really took a bath. They should have returned my calls.

In a nutshell, this scenario was played out thousands and thousands of times across America over the past three years. Banks finally collectively got the message, got smart(er) and decided that cutting some homeowners a little slack was clearly in their best financial interest. Rather than spending all that money to end up with a full portfolio of REO (real estate owned) inventory, they started talking. It was too late for me, but something tells me that even in their most generous moment, my bank would not have considered a $200,000 break on my mortgage balance. My child's children would most likely not live to see that house regain its full value.

Interested in how I know all this current information on housing values? While I was still in the house, I registered to received e-mail updates on my house with E-PROPERTY WATCH (www.EpropertyWatch.com). This great tool has kept me up-to-date on not only the value of my old house, but all recent and current bank/foreclosure actions in the area immediately surrounding my old subdivision. It was heartbreaking to see all those little red dots popping up in the e-mails, indicating more and more legal actions in the area. Clearly, even in my own small lake neighborhood, I was not alone.

Remember my wonderful friend Gary? He was the one who so graciously took the news back in 2008 that I wouldn't be able to pay on the business loan I had with his bank. And remember his comment at that time that "no one would even remember my small $50,000 business loan in a few years, as this situation was going to get significantly worse". Boy, was he right...more right than even he realized at the time.

Like many banks in the booming years of rising housing prices, Gary's bank was heavily invested in real estate, both commercial and residential. So heavily invested that their holdings to losses ratios caught the attention of the FDIC. After many grueling months of reporting, government overseeing and monitoring and staring into the face of the abyss, the FDIC took over his bank in the fall of 2011. He was given a 60 day notice that his position was eliminated from the bank that he had borrowed money to help fund.

Georgia now leads the nation in failed banks, with a count of 24 banks taken over by the FDIC in 2011 alone. The hunter becomes the hunted.

CHAPTER 12

"Paperback Writer"

Making a Living...No Matter What!

So, life went on for my son and me. In the spring of 2009, we had a new house (a brand new 4 bedroom house!), a 2005 Jaguar and I had a new job. After months & months of looking, I had landed a job in a dental office working for a woman who absolutely despised me. No really...not exaggerating. Despised.

As a consultant running a management company for several dental practices, she would breeze in once a week for her billed visit and never even speak to me. Never even made eye contact with me. It was hell, but it was a job. After decades of six figure incomes, I was leaving home at 5:45 a.m. to drive an hour to the most hostile work environment I had ever experienced...all for $17 an hour.

I did have one other job offer prior to accepting the dental office position I should tell you about. I had seen an ad somewhere that Skillpath, an international business seminar company was looking for trainers. The interview process involved multiple phone calls culminating in materials being sent from which I had to develop, practice and present a twenty minute video session submitted via YouTube. Not sure which was harder for me...developing the material or figuring out how to make a YouTube video!!

I submitted the video and waited. And then I got the call! I was so excited, until I found out that yet another step in the interview process involved preparing yet another session—this time to be delivered live via Skype to a team of hiring managers at the company. Oh boy...

The day of the scheduled interview came and I presented. The feedback seemed positive, and I got the call the following day that I had made the cut! I was ecstatic! I've delivered lots of training seminars in my time and I really enjoyed it. (Remember, I started out as a school teacher!!). Further, this job involved travel... something that I had been unable to do now that I was so broke. In the end, I thought I had finally landed the job that I could really start over with!

The final step was to fly to their corporate offices near Kansas City for an intensive week long training that would christen me as an official trainer (1099 status, not an employee). I could hardly wait! A few days later, I sat listening on a conference call covering the specifics of this new position. All travel expenses would be covered, a per diem dollar amount would cover meals & incidentals, and total compensation would be based largely on the amount of materials/books sold to the attendees of each seminar. It would be performance based, a lot of hard work and involved a great deal of travel (4-5 day long seminars per week). Nothing new or scary to me.

But there was a hitch (isn't there ALWAYS a hitch??) My mouth dropped open when they covered the travel reimbursement policy. All travel expenses were to be paid out of pocket by the individual (yes, that would be ME!). Receipts were to be submitted monthly and reimbursements averaged between thirty and forty-five days. They estimated that a credit card with a limit of a minimum of $10,000 was necessary.

Credit card!!! Access to $10,000??? I didn't have access to $1,000!! And despite the rumors you may have heard about credit card companies immediately chasing you with offers as soon as your bankruptcy is adjudicated proved to be completely false in my case (maybe because I didn't have a job??). In any case, it appeared to me that what was required was unattainable.

I explored every option. Would someone co-sign a credit card with me? Of course not...would you?? Even if I could muster a way to have access to some cash, I discovered that many car rental companies will not rent to you with a debit card. And without a credit card, hotels would debit a large amount at check in (vs. Just a small deposit with a credit card), so the amount of money I would need access to would be insurmountable. I tried every angle...all to no avail.

So with an EXTREMELY heavy heart, I phoned the company to tell that that I couldn't accept the position. While they were disappointed, they had no intention of making any exceptions to make it possible. Another career option bit the dust.

So you can see why I was so grateful for the dental office job. Even that small paycheck allowed my son and I to take the first real vacation we had taken in years. Using points earned through opening two new checking accounts with my bank and using the attached debit cards for every conceivable purchase over several months, I was able to accumulate enough miles to book two trips anywhere in the continental United States. I chose a point as far away as possible and booked us to San Francisco that summer to take advantage of my first paid vacation in 14 years!

Now remember, I had no credit card,, so I booked our hotel stay on Hotwire, allowing me to prepay our entire stay and reducing the amount of debit the hotel would take out of my checking account as a deposit when we checked in.

My son and I arrived at SFO on Saturday afternoon and took public transportation into the city (knowing how tough it was to rent a car without a credit card). We walked from the hotel to China town for dinner and strolled through a few shops on the way back. An inexpensive pocket knife caught my son's attention and I decided to treat him. Imagine my horror when the clerk came back to tell me in broken English that my card had been declined! I made her show me the receipt, because I couldn't believe it! I thought I was going to pass out! This debit card was the key to the only money I had in the world—the few hundred dollars that sat in my checking account. We put the knife back and began racing back to the hotel.

My son kept asking what was wrong. I told him I just had to get back to the hotel to see if we could reach someone at the bank. It was now Saturday early evening back home. My heart was in my mouth. I had less than $100 in cash, a debit card that held access to the only money I had in the world that was no worthless and I had little hope that I would be able to reach a live person at my bank on a Saturday night.

As we walked briskly, my son asked me in a very small voice, "Is this bad?" Knowing how hard it would be to reach someone and filling with dread at what the problem might be, I said, "Yes, it's bad. We need to get back to the hotel." He turned to me as we were walking and just the beginning of tears started to well up in his eyes. "Is this like losing our house bad?" His life...and his perspective about how bad things could get...had clearly been irrevocably altered by all we had been through in the last few years. And at that moment, barely breathing, I couldn't reassure him.

In the end, it was all okay. The crack fraud team at the bank had seen our dinner charge at a San Francisco restaurant and immediately put a security hold on the account. Fortunately for me, that team works 24/7 and I was able to get someone on the phone, clearing things up within ten minutes. But not before my son and I had been transported back to that horrible place where we had nothing.

Oh, and that job I hated so much? A few months later, this woman who despised me so much finally came in and called me to the back for a meeting. I told her that I knew she didn't want me there and asked her how we could resolve the situation. Her response was to fire me on the spot...right there with no notice! I cleaned out my drawer and drove home that Thursday afternoon, headed for my son's football game and wondering what would happen next.

Turns out that I had held that job just long enough to collect unemployment for the first time in my life! Remember, when all this happened to me, I had been self-employed for over 13 years. There is no collecting unemployment when the job you created for yourself goes away. But now I was eligible...and the amount I would eventually collect was only slightly less than the amount I had been making getting up at 5 a.m. to go to a job that I hated! Sometimes it is a great system!

And that woman who hated me so much? Turns out it really wasn't my imagination! I had become the 'go to' person in the office, but she refused to acknowledge that with any additional authority or money. But as fate would have it, she had been embezzling money from each of the dental offices that she was being paid to "manage". Everything from double billing consultant fees to using company credit cards for lavish trips she was forever taking her family on...she had been helping herself to the businesses tills. No wonder she didn't want me to have access to her books!

So yet another blessing in disguise. I've had more than I can name. It is clear to me now that God has had His hand in my life every step along the way...even when I felt like I was floating off into oblivion.   The big lesson for me??......"Let go and let God". And that is not easy for a type A control freak like me. But I'm getting stronger in my belief that there is a plan...a power even stronger than I think I am...walking along with me every single day of my life ☺

CHAPTER 13

"It's Been a Hard Day's Night"

Ain't It the Truth???

THE NEW NORMAL

Life has changed for everyone in the years since my tragic little story began. Being broke is now sort of strangely 'in vogue'. Spending money without regard is considered gouache. Admitting that you are cutting back and living leaner is not only acceptable—it is sort of expected, even for the wealthy. No scarlet letter for bankruptcy anymore.

Business has changed as well. Most companies have jumped on the bandwagon of austerity, doing more with less people and resources, etc., etc. My belief is that the wave of layoffs across America became so pervasive that nearly every large company/organization saw it as an opportunity to perform layoffs that they may not have done otherwise. Even food banks have filed for bankruptcy.

And as it always does, the pendulum swung completely to the opposite extreme in the banking industry. Even folks with excellent credit ratings are finding it difficult to obtain new mortgages...or even refinance an existing one. Banks that received bail out money have become hoarders, restructuring money flow to nearly a dead stop.

And big business has become the enemy. 'Too big to fail' has become a war chant for the masses. Class action law suits have arisen from the victims of devious bank practices. An example of this is the practice of large banks to 'order' checks and debits, causing the largest to be paid first out of an individual account every day. No problem, until you find yourself in an overdraft situation. Then a $20 balancing error could result in hundreds of dollars in overdraft charges. Imagine being overdrawn by $20, having the bank intentionally pay the largest debit first...say a $400 check...then letting every other debit that day (even a $2 Coke at the convenience store) ring up a hefty $35 bank fee.

Legislation has now been passed to make 'ordering' a thing of the past. And some of us in the class action suits may actually get a few dollars returned—while the attorneys make millions.

In the aftermath of the Great Recession, people are beginning to find their feet again. Social media has been the great leveler, even bringing malevolent leaders, of both business and governments, to their knees. Empires have fallen...it is Power to the People again!

As for me, I am still plugging along. Unemployment gave me the time and head start that I needed to get back to trying to create my own living. Jobs come and go, but it's hard to keep an entrepreneur down.

I now run a company that brings health fairs and employee events into corporations, schools and local governments. I've been at it now for a while and have established enough of a reputation that we operate mostly from referrals. I am not wealthy by ANY stretch of the imagination, but I now have a decent credit score of 727 and have even been approved for a couple of credit cards.

I'm turning my hard earned lessons into helping others by becoming a member of "Team Clark Howard". You may recall that I have loved Clark Howard for years (his cheap lifestyle philosophy anyway!) Now I am a weekly volunteer on his staff, taking phone calls and e-mails from his listeners who are currently living some of the same horrors that I have managed to survive. What good is a lesson learned if you can't pass it on??

I am also now serving on the board of a local United Way agency that helped me when my lights were about to be turned off. Back in the day, I led my church's mission initiatives and was the liaison for our charitable giving to this organization. Now I am a board member involved in their fund raising initiatives. Seems like life has come full circle in yet another way.

I still drive that 2005 Jaguar that I was approved for on the very day that the repo man was in my driveway, looking for the car that I was unable to reaffirm in my bankruptcy. And my friend Gary? He found a new job consulting with another bank that is under scrutiny by the FDIC. Perfect...he's got exactly the experience they need!

Before his bank went under last fall, I had been helping him try to package and sell a couple of investments he needed to get rid of. In the end, the deal that I put together fell through, but he felt that he wanted to do something to say thank you. One day we were having lunch and I was telling him how much I missed that little Miata convertible...the one on the cover that I had to sell to pay for my bankruptcy. When a Porsche pulled up, we admired it...and I told him that I had always dreamed of owning one. He told me that if I could find one that I could afford, he would co-sign the loan for me so I could get approved. Unbelievable.

Needless to say, I now am the proud owner of a very fast 2001 Porsche Boxster convertible. I drive it even when it is too cold to be driving a convertible....always with the top down!!

Many things have changed for me. Some relationships have come.....and others have gone away. But I have grown to a much deeper understanding of myself, learning that my internal barometer is a much better compass than whatever way the wind is blowing.

If I can only remember to stay true to myself, I believe that I still have lots to accomplish in this life...and lots of living to do!

So stay positive, love much, laugh often....and don't whine. Life is simply too short to allow it, no matter what your circumstances ☺